SEARCH

OTHER BOOKS BY JAMES KAVANAUGH

SEARCH

A Guide for Those Who Dare to Ask of Life Everything Good and Beautiful

James Kavanaugh

1817

Harper & Row, Publishers, San Francisco
Cambridge, Hagerstown, New York, Philadelphia
London, Mexico City, São Paulo, Singapore, Sydney

FIRST EDITION

Library of Congress Cataloging in Publication Data
Kavanaugh, James J.
    Search: a guide for those who dare to ask of life everything good and beautiful.

    1. Conduct of life. I. Title.
BJ1581.2.K355   1985   158   85–42781
ISBN 0-06-251803-8

85 86 87 88 89 HC 10 9 8 7 6 5 4 3 2 1

To Philip R. Kavanaugh, M.D., Frank Manley, Ph.D., and in memory of Robert E. Kavanaugh, Ph.D., who played such a significant part in the development of these ideas.

To fellow Searchers everywhere, especially to those who in workshops across the country have added to my own growth and understanding.

Contents

Preface

More than a decade ago I wrote a book of poetry called *There Are Men Too Gentle To Live Among Wolves*. In the Introduction I first admitted to being a *searcher*.

I am one of the *searchers*. There are, I believe, millions of us. We are not unhappy, but neither are we really content. We continue to explore life, hoping to uncover its ultimate secret. We continue to explore ourselves, hoping to understand. . . . This is a book for wanderers, dreamers, lovers, for lonely men and women who dare to ask of life everything good and beautiful.

These words reflected the feelings of one who had begun a long, difficult, and often lonely transition from one way of life to another. I had recently left the Catholic priesthood and begun a new life. I had left not furtively or quietly, but crying out in anguish in *A Modern Priest Looks at His Outdated Church*. I felt that the Church of my childhood had betrayed the docile trust of millions of faithful members and was failing in its mission to meet my own needs and those of countless others who had served so generously and well.

HOW SEARCH BEGAN

The response to this Introduction was startling and people wrote and continue to write from all over the English-speaking world admitting similar feelings. Many asked for help and guidance in their own "search" because my words offered them permission to begin. For some time I was not certain what to do, but a few years ago, when three of my brothers suddenly and successively died of cancer, I faced a deep and painful conflict that tore my life apart and broadened my own awareness of human suffering.

I looked for help in books, in therapy, even in medication. Although I found some help, my need was more profound. It was as if I had to reconstruct my whole value and support system. My ego was bruised and dying; my self-esteem had reached the bottom. No therapeutic pep talk could give me the strength and insight to go on. I was not looking for a quick fix. I was looking for a solid path, no matter the effort and time it took, that would place my life on an unshakable foundation. I prayed; I meditated; I reflected for hours on end. I tried any program that promised to take away my pain. Gradually I realized that for me there was no simple solution.

Finally I contacted my brother Philip, an outstanding psychiatrist in northern California who had been in private and group practice for more than twenty years. He always had a way of cutting to the heart of the matter with few words. I discovered that he was experiencing the same emotional and spiritual devastation I was. He and I and an insightful associate and friend, Dr. Frank Manley, who was experiencing a somewhat similar crisis in his own life, agreed to spend several weeks together carefully formulating ideas to ease our own pain, and to free ourselves from profound suffering that often left us frightened and helpless. Our personal struggle ultimately led to the formulation of the twelve principles of survival and personal growth that comprise the *Search Workshop* and form the substance of this book.

We started logically, by examining our own lives to decide what truths had been helpful or hurtful in our lifelong quest for a full and satisfying existence. What had happened to us? What course of action had helped us in the past? What mistakes and misconceptions had left us lonely and empty and unprepared for the present crisis, facing a kind of pain that we had never really experienced before. Developing and applying the *Search* principles, we began to gain greater self-knowledge, acquire a more solid faith in ourselves, and make increasing progress in finding freedom and direction.

THE TWELVE PRINCIPLES

The principles we came up with are not subtle or complex, but they cover all the basic aspects of living. The first three

Search principles deal with personal identity: (1) We must learn to be in touch with our *feelings* because our feelings tell us who we really are and to ignore them keeps us out of touch with our genuine self. (2) We must recognize our *dependencies* on others to discover if we are living honestly as ourselves or in a kind of self-imposed prison, living up to someone else's expectations out of desperation. (3) It is most important that we make a list of the *needs* in our lives that are not being met; otherwise we are angry and deprived, even slowly dying, and often have nothing to give anyone else.

The second group of *Search* principles deals with personal freedom: (4) Do we have genuine *options* in our lives or do we live with fantasies and impossible illusions that prevent growth? (5) Can we make necessary *decisions*, which are the raw material of real growth, or do we linger forever in painful, destructive indecision? (6) At the root of all of our actions and opinions lie our *belief systems*, most of which we well may have inherited. If they remain frozen beyond change or examination, personal development remains stagnant.

The third group of *Search* principles covers practical methods of personal growth: (7) Have we established solid *support systems* that can carry us through the various passages of life and times of crisis or painful and unexpected transitions? (8) Are we ready to *take risks* that will keep us in a positive and creative cycle of growth, or do we live with paralyzing fears? (9) Do we strive to *live in the present* rather than regret the past or focus on future anxieties, thus missing most of life?

The final group of *Search* principles is concerned with personal happiness: (10) How well do we *communicate?* Do we really listen? Are we really being heard? Communication is the core of all relationships. (11) Do we free ourselves from *negative people and situations* that deplete our energy? (12) Do we live with *passion and commitment* and make consistent contact with the *Spiritual Power* that resides within our innermost being?

After we had formulated and tested the ideas on ourselves, even though we were still healing, we began giving *Search Workshops* nearly five years ago. We did not want the groups to be threatening or abrasive, attacking or judgmental, because such approaches had not benefited us. The twelve principles are twelve concepts that apply to daily and long-term growth. Their value depends upon each individual's personal commitment to face life as it is—with persistence and patience, humility and laughter.

NOT THERAPY

Search is not therapy. The *Search Workshop* provides the context of a supportive group, a living, growing community of other gentle people. Thus *Search* is a positive, supportive program, for active, basically healthy people who are in a difficult passage or painful transition: ending or beginning a relationship, seeking or exploring a new way of life, confronting aging and death, changing jobs, altering a lifestyle, establishing a new identity that better reflects one's self, finding new meaning in a life grown dull, or discovering a new way of living because previous methods that worked for years are no longer effective.

Change, though often painful, can be an opportunity to increase joy and energy, to foster self-esteem and strengthen confidence, and to build a solid personality base. If we understand and apply healthy principles of human growth, we can view our painful depression or anxiety or fatigue as telling us that we *cannot* live as we have in the past. What once held us together and gave us self-confidence no longer does. If we are to live, we *must* change. And if we are to change, we must find guidance and direction.

SEARCH WORKSHOPS

When I began taking *Search* on the road, the results in various sectors of the country were more than exciting. Many participants found *Search* one of the most important weekends of their lives, precisely because it does not end after a weekend. It begins a way of life tailored to an individual's own needs. My years of experience in writing and counseling have led me to believe that only a positive energy and atmosphere are ultimately effective in human growth. The very lack of energy is what keeps us depressed, anxious, insecure, and afraid.

After I had traveled the country and had honed the twelve principles through practical experience in the groups and sensed their power in my own life, I felt eager to share *Search* in written form. I wanted to capture the essence of the principles so that those unable to take a *Search Workshop* could have access to them. This book will also give those planning to attend an idea of what *Search* is all about and afterward provide a complete and solid reminder of the experience for those who have attended, reinforcing the long-range effects of the program.

NO INSTANT CURE

These principles are not miraculous or the source of an instant cure. I am no longer looking for an instant cure. I have tried too many. Now I am at times joyful and confident, and at other times still struggling for my own peace, joy, contentment, and direction. Nor are the principles particularly subtle or new, but when practiced consistently they can have a profound and lasting impact. The art of living can be learned like any other skill. Thus *Search* is not a fleeting, emotional experience, but a basic, practical understanding of the dynamics of human growth. Many of us continue to make the same mistakes in dealing with life decisions and repeat destructive patterns that deplete energy. We refuse to take risks that can save our lives; we even ask God to do for us what we must do for ourselves. I am convinced that searchers need direction and support. They have the life force, the courage, the faith, and the determination to discover in life all that is good and beautiful. Often they only lack a plan.

It is my hope that *Search* can be that plan—a systematic guide to self-awareness, a course that teaches us how to approach life. Most of us never learned about life except through trial-and-error experience. Experience and a private, lonely struggle are not enough for most of us. But experience and *Search* can provide solid and successful direction for personal growth.

A LIFE PLAN

I have often been inspired by other books and workshops for a few hours or days. *Search* tries to develop a solid life plan that endures. Yet this program is not gospel. You can modify these ideas to create your own plan, to play the "long game" and create the kind of world you deserve. Friends can help, but no one else, no matter how loving, can really do it for us, and change takes effort and time. This may be hard to accept, but when we cease looking for a savior outside ourselves, we discover the healing spirit of the God or Power within. This book seeks to share what many of us have learned in our personal odysseys. There are millions of people in the throes of an individual life struggle who need the strength and support of *Search* and other *Searchers*. Often there is no place to go other than into private therapy, which does not work for everyone, or a medical facility, which can render one more hopeless and frightened than before.

I am convinced that this book can be of great help to those persons like me who, at times, experience the loneliness and depression, the confusion and isolation, the emptiness and vague unrest of a searcher who refuses to live in a prison, no matter how secure and comfortable, or those like me who have ignored their own feelings out of guilt or pseudoresponsibility and feel a gnawing awareness that they want much more from life than it presently offers.

EPIDEMIC OF PAIN

I am increasingly aware that spiritual and emotional pain have reached epidemic proportions in our society. But because the deeply lonely and wounded continue to get out of bed and meet their responsibilities, no one really pays them any real heed. They can be young, or old, or struggling through mid-life confusion. They can be rich or poor, busy or idle, lawyer or psychologist, married or single, involved or reclusive. Often they live in relationships that have lost their fire, work at even lucrative jobs that do not represent or fulfill them, this despite the fact that today they have options never before possible.

Like me, they may have struggled, studied, wondered, sought medical and other professional help, read widely, succeeded and failed, started and ended relationships, and trusted devoutly the fantasies of our culture that power and financial success will bring us joy and peace. At times they can ignore the pain or bury the feelings that lie just beneath the surface. They work harder, drink more, jog more assiduously, talk more incessantly, pursue sex or other relationships more compulsively, and hope that some magic will heal their distress. But often, as in my own case, a time of crisis bares the sadness and boredom, the anger, anxiety, depression, or despair that binds them deep inside. And then they do not know where to turn. I believe *Search* can offer them a new and effective way to live the rest of their lives.

Some turn in despair to illicit drugs, divorce, alcohol, or any possible kind of instant cure. Or they may simply struggle silently in a kind of slow suicide, finally sharing their profound struggle with no one. They have lost their lust for life despite their apparent and superficial success. *Search* offers an overview of life that can help them to understand what has gone wrong and what they can do about it.

I want this book, born of a lifetime of my own joy and pain, anxiety and courage, depression and confidence, anger and hurt and love, to be a personal gift, a bright ray of enlightenment and hope to the thousands of searchers who "dare to ask of life everything good and beautiful."

Introductory Note

In each chapter I capture as well as I can the basic material used in the *Search Workshops*. The stories reveal the kind of sharing that some individuals offer in response to the principles. Naturally, I have taken pains to protect their privacy. No one is ever pushed or forced to talk, as they might be in a therapy group. Occasionally included are some exercises I have found helpful in developing a deeper understanding of the principles, and at the end of the chapters are axioms to help keep the principles firmly in mind.

I again emphasize that *Search* is for healthy individuals who seek personal growth and are moving through some transition in their lives. It may well improve a relationship, but it seeks primarily to assist an individual man or woman to achieve fullness of life.

I make liberal use of poetry since, as is now widely recognized in therapeutic circles, poetry has a unique way of touching the core of a feeling with an economy of words and a depth of universal understanding. It also offers a gentle, relaxing change of pace. *Search* is a lifelong journey, and intensity or the hope of an instant cure can cloud our vision and impede the fullness of perception that occurs in a relaxed atmosphere. All of the poetry I quote is my own.

Regardless of anything else, I hope this book can be an important step in self-discovery, in understanding the dynamics of personal growth and happiness. I really believe we can make our life what we want it to be. We can have the kind of relationship and work that is most fulfilling, and we can discover the personal mission that is truly our destiny. I don't think that for most of us it is a simple task, but with patience and determination we can create our own world and the kind of life that fulfills our deepest dreams.

Few of us have not been wounded by even those who love us. We feel pushed to excel, are frequently dissatisfied with our best efforts, compare ourselves to others as the measure of our worth, or are pushed to live our lives for someone else. *Search* offers a way out, a path of freedom to discover ourselves no matter how late in the game it may seem to be. The pain will go away; the light will shine; the rhythm and balance will be restored. Spontaneity and creativity will again be the energizing force of our lives. We only must dare to ask for "everything good and beautiful."

PERSONAL IDENTITY

There are men too gentle to live among wolves
Who prey upon them with IBM eyes
And sell their hearts and guts for martinis at noon.
There are men too gentle for a savage world
Who dream instead of snow and children and Halloween
And wonder if the leaves will change their color soon.

There are men too gentle to live among wolves
Who anoint them for burial with greedy claws
And murder them for a merchant's profit and gain.
There are men too gentle for a corporate world
Who dream instead of candied apples and ferris wheels
And pause to hear the distant whistle of a train.

There are men too gentle to live among wolves
Who devour them with eager appetite and search
For other men to prey upon and suck their childhood dry.
There are men too gentle for an accountant's world
Who dream instead of Easter eggs and fragrant grass
And search for beauty in the mystery of the sky.

There are men too gentle to live among wolves
Who toss them like a lost and wounded dove.
Such gentle men are lonely in a merchant's world,
Unless they have a gentle one to love.

From *There Are Men Too Gentle to Live Among Wolves*

1. We Are Our Feelings

Principle One: *Discover what you are feeling, accept your feelings without editing. Your feelings are you.*

I remember clearly the day I left home at fifteen to begin my studies for the priesthood. A family photo reminds me. I stood by the family car with my older brother, already a seminarian, and my mother. My brother looked almost happy. My mother seemed radiant. I was on the verge of tears, but I would not release them. It wasn't allowed.

I didn't really want to leave home, but I had been destined for the priesthood since childhood. I had been taught that when God calls, I must obey. I never heard God's call, but everyone else heard it for me and I felt helpless. The priests in our parish had assured me for years that I was priestly material. The nuns gave me the benign smile reserved for future priests. My mother, who had once wanted to be a nun herself, prayed every day for my vocation. Our home seemed almost part of the Church. We went to daily Mass and evening services, recited the rosary daily, and often entertained priests in our home. The Church was our whole life, and I was a shy, smiling boy who went along with the program. I didn't know what else to do. Even my grade-school classmates knew that I was destined for the priesthood and excluded me from "dirty" stories and kissing games.

In a sense, it was an easy way out. I did not have to make decisions about the future. I could avoid any adolescent conflict with sex and hide my persistent fear of women. And I was guaranteed instant prestige. I had served Mass since I was six, Latin and all, and to enter the seminary was only to graduate from being an altar boy. My life was established and I only had to live

3

it out. But beyond the docile smile, there was a seething cauldron of feelings I was afraid to express.

I had a secret side I shared with no one except my dog. We spent thousands of hours wandering in a wonderful woods a few blocks from my Michigan home. No one else was privy to my private world of fantasy, where I could be a forest ranger, a bush pilot, a star baseball player, a coach, a veterinarian, but never a priest. In school plays I always was in Roman collar. So when I left for the seminary, I abandoned my dog, the woods, and my rich world of fantasy to please others. It was not the only time I ignored my feelings.

I had also suppressed my feelings on the football field. I was good at the game but I hated the calisthenics, the pain and drudgery of daily practice, the stink of the filthy locker room, and the terror of tackling a rugged body twice the size of my own to prove my "guts." Football was the prescribed rite of passage to manhood in my world, the proof of my worth, so I ignored my feelings and subjected myself to the fierce scrimmages during the glorious Indian summers of Michigan. I longed to be wandering with my dog, startling snakes and rabbits and porcupines, and dreaming private dreams of adventure, but I had been well taught to ignore my feelings. Feelings were suspect, self-indulgent, weak. It was discipline and will power that mattered. I made every effort to please those who loved me so they would not abandon their love. Years later I wrote a poem that described my feelings. The poem erupted from nowhere; it was as if it wrote itself. Long after I had left the priesthood, I was able to know who I was without prolonged therapy telling me it was okay. Finally I could be myself.

I knew this skinny little kid
Who never wanted to play tackle football at all,
But thought he'd better if he wanted his daddy to love him
    And to prove his courage and things like that.

I remember him holding his breath and closing his eyes
    And throwing a block into a guy twice his size,
Proving he was brave enough to be loved and crying softly

Because his tailbone hurt and his shoes were so big they made him
stumble.

I knew this skinny little kid with sky blue eyes
    And soft brown hair, who liked cattails and pussy willows,
Sumac huts and sassafras, chestnuts and pine cones, and oily walnuts,
Lurking foxes and rabbits munching lilies,
Secret caves and moss around the roots of oaks,
Beavers and muskrats and gawking herons,
And I wonder what he would have been
    If someone had loved him for just following the fawns,
And building waterfalls, and watching the white rats have babies.
I wonder what he would have been if he hadn't played tackle football
    at all.

From Will You Be My Friend?

It was twenty years after the fact that I was able to write that
poem, because only then was I free enough to be aware of my
real feelings. It was then, too, that I acknowledged I had never
wanted to be a priest. I wanted to help others somehow; I was
filled with all the best in youthful idealism and had a tremendous sense of adventure, but I did not want to be a priest. The
oppressive years spent in the seminary were largely sad and depressing when I was alone with my private thoughts, but no one
ever knew because I hid my unhappiness under the shy smile. I
learned to compete intensely in sports and studies until my
whole value as a person depended on my achievements; my life
was not spontaneous and rhythmic. It was a lesson that would
take a lifetime to unlearn.

Why? I had trampled on my feelings. I was not living the way
I wanted to live. Sexual feelings became sinful thoughts.
Dreams of another kind of life were temptations. Resentment
of authority and childish rules was dangerous pride. I struggled
to be kind, patient, pure, docile, and grateful for my holy vocation. All the while I ignored my feelings and became a stranger
to myself. During the summer at home, I was tense and nervous, easily provoked to tears as I continued to study, to avoid
girls and movies and all temptations. It never occurred to me
that I was out of sync with myself and everyone else—including

God. I struggled to become the person that others wanted me to be. My innermost feelings were smothered and life was not a search but an endless test, and my whole being protested.

There were numerous personal signs that I did not want to be in the seminary. Bad dreams, tension, growing introversion, tormented thoughts, frequent depression, and almost constant anxiety. But I felt I had no choice. God had called me. Years later I wrote about the "easy God" who only demanded that I keep the rules and please everyone but myself. I could write then because my feelings were no longer bottled up.

I have lost my easy God, the one whose name I knew since childhood,
    I knew his temper, his sullen outrage, his ritual forgiveness
I knew the strength of his arm, the sound of his insistent voice,
His beard bristling, his lips full and red with moisture
    at the moustache . . .
I never told him how he frightened me, how he followed me
    as a child when I played with friends
Or begged for candy on Halloween . . .
He the mysterious took all mystery away, corroded my imagination,
Controlled the stars and would not let them speak for themselves.

Now he haunts me seldom, some fierce umbilical is broken,
I live with my own fragile hopes and sudden rising despair.
Now I do not weep for my sins, I have learned to love them
And to know that they are the wounds that make love real . . .
I walk alone, but not so terrified as when he held my hand . . .
Now the world is mine with all its pain and warmth,
    With its every color and sound.
The setting sun is my priest with the ocean for his altar,
The rising sun redeems me with the rolling waves
    warmed in its arms . . .
I lie on the grass and boy-like search the sky.
The clouds do not turn to angels, the winds do not whisper
    of heaven and hell.
                    From *There Are Men Too Gentle to Live Among Wolves*

SEARCH DEALS WITH PRESENT FEELINGS

Search deals with present feelings and only those past feelings that are still being felt. We have to become aware of these feelings, even unpleasant ones, if we are ever to know who we really are. When we deny strong feelings as I did for twenty or thirty years, they take their toll at some point in bodily symptoms, disease, depression, or consistent unhappiness. Some people spend most of their lives working at a job they despise or living with a spouse they can't really endure. It may well be that a great number of people lead lives of "quiet desperation." I see it in lonely eyes every day. The young woman who sold me shirts yesterday at Penney's was darkly attractive and barely twenty-five. Yet her listless voice and posture, and especially her eyes, revealed the deep, wounding sadness and despair that wanted to scream out her pain. But she will not scream it out. She will dream of some magical solution, seek her release in novels or movies or the soaps, and join the parade of the empty and miserable.

SEARCHERS ASK MORE

Searchers refuse to live that way. They ask more of life. They want to remain in touch with their feelings, to discover a creative, energizing way of life that reflects who they really are— no matter how long it takes. They realize that bodily tension and other physical symptoms are a danger sign of suppressed feelings, the source of stress that can promote cancer or high blood pressure. Even bright, seemingly perceptive persons can deny what they are feeling for a very long time.

Dave, a respected young psychologist, admitted at a *Search Workshop* that he felt constant tension in his stomach and pain in his cheeks. For years he ignored these signs, accepting them as innate anxiety that had pursued him from childhood. Therapy had not helped, although he had gained a more rational understanding of his life. In *Search* we did not probe or analyze; he simply became increasingly aware of the severe tension in a deep breathing exercise and fantasy trip.

Dave's suppressed feelings are common. Like the rest of us,

he was taught in and outside the home what feelings were acceptable. As a boy he struggled to ignore fear and weakness, even as girls are usually taught to deny anger or feelings of violence. But the feelings didn't really go away no matter how much we prayed or denied them or pretended they didn't exist. They simply went underground, locked helplessly in our bodies, and prevented us from attaining any real self-knowledge.

Over a period of time, Dave recognized that he had never wanted to be a psychologist. He hated the work and realized that a well-meaning father had pushed him into the profession. The Ph.D. made Dave's father pay attention to him and feel proud of him. Dave's real interests centered on the outdoors, nature, and especially the ocean and its inhabitants. Scuba diving had been almost an addiction when time meant nothing and Dave's exuberance was at a peak. Even when he talked about it, his voice lost the flat, monotonous inflection and his eyes came alive. Psychology made him intense and serious and heavy, restless and depressed, and he had hoped that it would provide him with the key to his misery. Finally he recognized what had happened and when he decided to study oceanography, the pressure in his stomach and cheeks began to dissolve, his marriage improved, his sexual vitality returned, and a sullen grayness that had been his constant shadow began to fade.

THERAPY VERSUS SELF-HEALING

It is not always easy to find the connection between our pain and the feelings we have suppressed, but for reasonably healthy, active people it is more effective to "feel" our way to self-awareness than to analyze *ad nauseum*. Some of what passes for therapy is unnecessary and expensive. Frequently it creates the impression that there is some wise person who can find the solution to our problem when only we can do that. We are the answer and *Search* encourages us to take risks and to discover the way of self-healing. And self-healing begins with an awareness of what we are feeling. To know our feelings without editing or qualifying, without classifying them as good or bad.

There are good and bad therapists as there are good and bad members of any profession. Therapy can as often interfere with our growth as it can foster it. We have to decide. Although I have experienced my share of excellent therapy, some of it was a pointless effort to explore my early life to discover where I went wrong. I rehashed every shred of my existence until even I was bored—and with little personal growth. My parents, priests, and teachers did the best they could. I myself had known at a very young age that my personal subculture was debilitating, but I was too frightened to express my own innermost feelings at such a fragile age. The climate was not right. Curiously, those youthful perceptions never changed. I didn't need to know more about myself; I simply had to find the courage to act on what I had known for years.

Consequently, much of the therapy I took was a waste of time and money. I was looking for someone to do what I had to do for myself. Attacking my father's strictness or my mother's religiosity and insecurity told me nothing I did not already know. I finally had to become my own therapist, even when in therapy, and what has proved gradually helpful for me is contained in the principles of *Search*—beginning and ending with an awareness of my own feelings. This is obviously not to indict all of psychotherapy; it is merely to remove its magical component and make me retain responsibility for my own self-awareness and personal growth.

SEX AND FEELINGS

Sylvia, a thirty-four-year-old legal secretary, could never really enjoy sex. Her body became rigid, her vagina dry, and she felt cheap after any sexual experience. Raised in a strict religious background, she thought she had to clarify her own feelings about God and sin before she could enjoy sex. She went to a therapist. With him she relived her confessions for years. This was his need, not hers. He understood little about her faith and had adopted the cultural stereotype about the confessional. He would have done better to talk about foreplay or his vegetable garden, for that matter, because religion wasn't the problem. She simply felt sexually inadequate, awkward, and overweight and wondered if she could really please any lover. There was no need for endless sessions of analysis to extricate these feelings. They emerged spontaneously when she learned to be aware of and trust her own feelings rather than clinging to her confused thoughts and the therapeutic theories of a professional. By becoming acutely aware of the tensions in her body, she was able to "feel" her way to the connection between bodily feelings and personal inadequacy. She stopped blaming a seventh-grade nun and recognized her own fear of a bad sexual performance.

Ken, a middle-aged stockbroker, gentle and humorous, had married a woman with two children. He began to feel immense tension in his hands and chest and sought help alternately for arthritis and high blood pressure. When he began to get in touch with his feelings, he recognized the increased pressure occurred whenever his seven-year-old stepson was present. He deeply resented the boy, who invaded the master bedroom unannounced and constantly demanded his mother's attention. When Ken was present the boy only whispered to his mother. Gradually Ken saw the connection between his deep anger and outrage and his personal stress. What he was going to do about it was up to him. *Search's* part was to help him recognize what a trusted friend his body is, what an accurate barometer of suppressed feelings, and to realize that his true feelings establish his personal identity no matter how controlled and patient he may seem outwardly.

FEELINGS ARE TO BE FELT

This first principle is absolutely vital if *Search* is not to be an introductory psychology class or an intellectual discussion about feelings. Feelings are to be felt! We can try to talk them away, drink or smoke them away, laugh or shout them away, or, more often, retreat from them through denial, but they will wait patiently to cripple us physically or emotionally as long as we reject our very identity as a person. If our image of ourselves refuses us the right to be angry or even unpleasant, our own kindness will probably kill us. Or if our self-image prevents us from being gentle and soft and even afraid, we will wall ourselves off from the world in a private tomb. *Searchers* must *feel* to grow, to understand, to become who they were destined to be. Feelings are not good or bad; they simply are. They do not lie to us or play games with us. Ideologies can do that and our minds have had much practice at it. Our minds are capable of vanity, distortion, and deceit; our feelings are not. If we reject them, they will not disappear. They will only go underground and rip us apart. We may call it a stroke or cancer or depression, but it is more than likely a long-term denial of feelings. We pay massive attention to the effects of nicotine, sugar, alcohol, narcotics, cholestrol, and infrequent exercise, but corroded feelings are the great murderers and millions of people barely understand them.

I am not suggesting that we act on every feeling; I am talking about awareness. We can feel rage without killing someone. More than likely impulsive killers have no awareness of their rage. We can feel extreme jealousy without smashing windows or reading someone else's mail. There was a time in the sixties when feelings seemed to be "discovered" and therapy programs seemed to dictate that all feelings be expressed. I can remember when it was difficult to attend a cocktail party in southern California without getting a drink poured down your shirt. There are numerous situations when it is not suitable to express our feelings, but it is still terribly important to be aware of them.

FEELINGS AND PARENTAL FIGURES

Julaine, a buyer for a large department store, admitted that her mother has been dying of "something" for the last twenty years. A conversation with this parent is like going for a romantic walk in a wind tunnel. If she does not have endless physical problems, she has a well-memorized list of everyone who has neglected, insulted, attacked, or ignored her. When Julaine calls, the first five minutes are devoted to why she didn't call sooner. Julaine has tried innumerable times, directly and indirectly, to tell her mother that she is self-centered, narrow, depressing, boring, and hostile. She has also tried hugging her, praising her, and buying her gifts, but her mother never changes. Apparently she doesn't want to change or doesn't know how. If Julaine doesn't want to stagger away from every conversation as if she had been pummeled by a leopard, she has to deal with her mother in a different way. Either she avoids all contact or she refuses to cater to her mother's litany of woes. To share her own feelings with her mother seems a waste of time. Talking to her about anything is an emotional disaster. *Search* did not solve Julaine's problem. It simply helped her become aware of what she was really feeling and taught her that she was not alone in her struggle. She can solve her own problem if she chooses to.

There are other situations when financial pressure makes it difficult to express feelings. Barbara works for a neurosurgeon who treats her like an ignorant teenager. He is arrogant, rude, overbearing, dictatorial, and totally insensitive, but since she is the sole support of two young children she needs the job. She fears to risk telling the doctor what she feels, so she is secretly looking for another job.

On the other hand, Dolores, a bank executive, hesitated to express her feelings to a petty vice-president whose grossly cruel remarks kept her in a constant rage.

"Nothing ever suits him. He laughs at women even though I do most of his work. Without me he couldn't get his job done. At first I was able to ignore his rudeness and obscene remarks, but over the months, I've wanted to kill him. I just can't stand it!"

Dolores knew that the bank needed her and that she could

find another good job without difficulty. *Search* helped her to clarify her rage. She confronted the offensive man without rancor and told him how he made her feel. Matters improved immeasurably the very same day.

SOME HIDE PERSONAL FEELINGS

Thousands of couples hide their personal feelings from one another and let them leak out in pique or nagging, or they retreat into an aggressive silence. Personal loneliness and hurt becomes a way of life. After months or years of unexpressed feelings, they do not know how to break down barriers. Often they settle for a silent hostility or a polite, superficial truce. There are a great number of people who can exist that way. They disappear into their own world and share only life's trivia. *Searchers* want a relationship to mean something or end.

THE LONG GAME

Search encourages us to play the "long game," to create step by step the kind of life we truly want. As *Searchers* we do not wait for some external approval to make our behavior acceptable, nor do we act impulsively. Impulsive behavior is often a refusal to experience a painful feeling that can help us to grow.

Darrell, a machinist, tall, sensitive, and extremely hard working, finally decided to leave his wife, Jennifer, because he constantly felt jealous. Because Jennifer was a college graduate, attractive, with a sensuous figure and pert manner that got attention, he was painfully troubled when any man talked to her personally. A friend's kiss or a hand on her shoulder during conversation was immediately noted and timed. He accused her of staring at other men's crotches or of having a fascination for any professional man. In reality, Jennifer was deeply in love with Darrell precisely because he was unpretentious and gentle, and she quietly denied his accusations. He reviewed her phone calls, considered any sweater too tight, searched her purse for notes or phone numbers, checked her mail, and quizzed the kids about any visitors. Jennifer continued to try vainly to reassure him. Finally he left her.

At *Search*, as he got minimally in touch with his feelings, he recognized his own desire for more education. He wanted his own body shop, but his preoccupying jealousy drained his energy. He was certain Jennifer would leave him and took the step before she could. He spent so much time wondering what kind of man turned her on that he had ignored his own needs. Psychiatric help taught him that his jealously stemmed from his mother's desertion of the family when he was eleven, but this awareness did not resolve his problem. He had not allowed himself to feel his own fear and dependence. In the workshop he was able to tell others about his near terror that he would lose his wife and family forever. He had been miserable since the breakup, watched her house at night, and waited for a man to walk out. The meter reader or an itinerant salesman could have been maimed. He talked about punching a man at a wedding reception who had kissed Jennifer, and then about the ensuing self-hatred he felt. He became aware that his jealousy moved him to attack rather than to express his self-doubts and personal fears. The attacks pushed Jennifer further away and left him feeling guilty and unlovable. It was a vicious cycle that gave his wife no chance to reassure and love him. Because he couldn't stand the self-loathing, he had finally run away. Once his real feelings became clear, he could begin the long process of recovery. There was no miracle but there was day-by-day progress.

TAKING RISKS

A *Searcher* feels the feeling and takes the risk of expressing it.

Theresa, a thin, sensitive brunette, was married to a man who lectured her constantly as if she were a naive child. Gradually she closed her ears and shut Greg out of her life. A large, powerful man and president of a meat-packing firm, he was not aware that he had intimidated his wife for years and treated her like just another employee. When he complained about their sex life, she admitted that she had turned him off emotionally. She told him that she felt he never listened, that she feared a physical attack if she disagreed, and that she wanted a job outside the home. She anticipated the lecture that would follow, but Greg seemed totally startled by her admission. A few months later she began working outside the home, made new friends, and felt a new respect from her husband. He almost stopped lecturing, or laughed when he caught himself, and became proud of what she had accomplished.

There is little reason to express our feelings if they will not be heard or will be ridiculed. And there is little sense in remaining in a relationship that prevents us from being ourselves. By playing the "long game," we focus on ourselves and make every honest effort to express who we are. If the situation remains toxic and unbearable, we are not afraid to terminate a relationship, change jobs, move to a new area, or alter our lifestyle—whatever it takes.

Searchers may even have to phase out impossible social charades, or they may discover that there are few "impossible" situations once they are able to be honestly themselves. Increasingly we discover we want to be ourselves in all circumstances of our lives and gradually create a total style of life where that is possible. It all begins with discovering our feelings without editing.

Anybody knows that the way to live life is to get married
To someone you like a lot, and to get a job you learn to do well.
To have kids you can worry about, to have friends and hobbies
    You like a lot—or usually.
Not to wander about like someone who's always changing his mind,
Wondering about life and not settling down—as they say—
Lonely a lot and hurting a lot between the joys.
Someone who feels from morning till night, and doesn't have
    Enough sense to believe
That he'll never find what he wants.

Who down deep is always afraid till he lets go of all the things
   He learned to hang on to.
Anybody knows
   Except someone like you—and me.
                              From *Sunshine Days and Foggy Nights*

FEELINGS AND DIVORCE

Many of us stumbled into our life's work or our marriage by accident. As we grow to experience our innermost feelings, we gradually recognize who we are and how we want to live. The tragedy of divorce might not be nearly as frequent if we learned to express our feelings from the very beginning. Most of us compromise our feelings early on. Gradually they are buried. Resentment and anger stealthily become hard and recalcitrant, hurt multiplies by its own square root until genuine communication seems impossible. Some stick it out "for the children" or out of passivity and ennui. *Searchers* take action no matter how long it takes because they realize that life is a series of new beginnings. They want to be in charge of their own life and to create all that is good and beautiful. This does not mean there is no pain, no tragedy, no real conflict. It means that tragedy and pain are confronted and felt as an integral part of a loving relationship. This is difficult when we lie about our feelings or ignore them from the start of a relationship and play an elaborate role. *Searchers* refuse to live like a lazy log floating down a river. To most:

Love is as much an accident as life, as much a mystery
   as death or pain,
As capricious and uncertain as the whims of a summer rain.
Love is what is at hand, a city where I happened to be born,
A tree or an acre of land, a friendly bed that kept me warm.
A hand that eased my hurt, a breast, a place to drop my pack, and rest.
Familiarity grown comfortable and more familiar.
   Love is life's refusal to be alone,
   Better an angry, silent home than all the darkness.
Love is whatever I want it to be, love is whatever it seems to me.

So many words explaining it, so many songs proclaiming it,
Only a rare and precious love is free.

From *Walk Easy on the Earth*

At the beginning of a *Search Workshop* I am usually faced with thirty or forty people I've never met. But as potential *Searchers*, I know they are risk takers who want to create life rather than to let it happen. Since I want the experience to be more than a passing shot in the arm, I encourage them to learn the principles, to apply them consistently, and to chart their own growth. Often I use a simple breathing exercise to help them get in touch with their feelings. I also take them on a childhood fantasy trip to enter a more spontaneous and uninhibited period of their lives. Once they can visualize themselves as a child, it helps for them to let that child emerge and hold the child lovingly in their own arms. This can also be most effective in the privacy of one's own home.

BREATH AND SPIRIT

Curiously, the Latin word for "breath" is *spiritus*. Thus the breath is the spirit of the body. Breath, passing through the tension of our body as spirit, makes us more conscious of our unity and feelings. That is why it is such a significant part of yoga and allied forms of healing. Most people are not aware of how powerful this tension, this blockage of feeling really is. Tension becomes so much a part of their existence that they learn to tolerate it.

A dozen years ago I engaged in an extreme therapeutic exercise that taught me how much tension I had stored to escape feelings. The therapy was called "process therapy," indicating by its name—much like *Search*—that growth takes place over our entire lives.

The therapy consisted of simply lying alone on a thin mattress in a private room and focusing on my body. I breathed deeply from my diaphragm in the yogic manner without hyperventilating. Gradually I began to feel physical tension in my cheeks, my neck, my stomach and legs, and my back. The therapist simply observed at intervals. I continued the process at home, abstaining from alcohol, sex, cigarettes, and TV. After a few days I felt such pain in my body I could barely tolerate it. The therapist told me that there were unexpressed emotions behind that physical pain.

Soon I got in touch with feelings that had been ignored for most of my life. I had been playing a brave, fearless man when I often felt like a scared little boy. I had allowed others to take my life away and buried the anger. My body ached for touching, for warmth, even as my heart ached for intimacy and love. When the feelings began to emerge, my body began to relax. There was a startling connectedness between body and spirit. I remained in the program for several weeks until it was difficult to distinguish between my sleeping and waking hours. Finally, it was enough and I gradually reintegrated myself into my world. I was not "cured," but I knew graphically and forever the massive tension of ignored feelings.

There is hardly enough that can be said for deep breathing from the diaphragm. A central part of the ancient Yoga experience, it is an antidote to every kind of tension and illness. I relax and extend the diaphragm as I inhale deeply through the nose, then draw the diaphragm toward the navel as I exhale through the mouth. Often it helps to count while breathing in and out, or to visualize a golden light passing through the entire body. In this way I rid myself of distracting, anxious thoughts and sink deeply into my own relaxed center of feelings.

In such an exercise we can cultivate a sense of "letting go," of surrendering to what is. So often we battle with ourselves, struggling to keep in place what must be abandoned. In the process of letting go, we have a deep faith in the integrity of our being, a faith that our body knows what we want and need. There is increasing evidence that we can be our own healers, that relief from stress and pain takes place in silence. As we practice the breathing exercise consistently, we begin to know who we really are and what we really want. The long-blocked feelings will be released and can be attended to.

At times, when I seem out of touch, I repeat the breathing process briefly and I encourage participants in the workshop to do the same. Most of them discover areas of tension and often are able to release them by entering their bodies and breathing out the stress. The areas of emotional tension vary widely: hands, thighs, neck, back, stomach, groin, chest, feet, cheeks, eyes, even knees. Discovering areas of tension offers an honest, infallible insight into the personality and can be the key to the secret chamber of locked emotions. We can even learn which tense area of the body is tied to which suppressed feeling.

When the group is relaxed, I go around the room and ask anyone who chooses to say something "good" about him- or herself. The second time around I ask them to say something "very good," to "boast," to express their most creative quality. I won't forget the young man who said he was the greatest sex partner in the world. Nor will I forget when I felt that way a couple of decades ago. This exercise helps form the group and puts us in the positive mode. It also can be done effectively by an individual or couple, or in an ad hoc group of other *Searchers*. The dynamic of healthy, searching people in support of one another seems to give individuals permission to enter areas of feeling that might have been denied them in other settings, or at least areas that did not seem quite real before in a more formal environment. The *Searchers* begin to recognize that there are many others who feel as they do. For many, it is the first time they have not felt terribly alone.

Many of us searchers have been considered odd, weird and irresponsible, unsettled or selfish, asking too much of life, independent, stubborn, wanderers, dreamers, or idealists doomed to isolation and unhappiness. It is always a great relief for me to meet other searchers, individuals who refuse to settle for routine boredom or a pointless, uncreative existence. Almost instinctively, I seek them out even in social situations. They want all that life has to offer and are willing to make any change to discover it. They will not accept docility and conformity in place of intimacy and love. And any honest and significant change begins with *feelings*. Without feeling, love is impossible, no matter how it appears.

Search begins and ends with feelings: love, hate, sadness, joy, anger, fear, loneliness, peace. It is our feelings that let us know who we are—not our appearance or degrees, our financial status or family, not even our job or friends, but how we *feel* about ourselves in relationship to all of these. And it is our present feelings, not our past ones. An absolutely gorgeous woman can feel fat and unattractive; a brilliant man can feel unsuccessful and average. One obese person is despondent and constantly preoccupied with dieting; another is vivacious, creative, and happy. Feelings make the difference. I remember as an adolescent when a single pimple could make me feel like a biblical leper.

STAYING IN THE PRESENT

Search does not probe past relationships. Any past feelings that are of significance still perdure in the present. The lonely child can still be present in the lonely man or woman, and thus holding and nurturing that child can be most helpful. We can unravel the events of our past life endlessly and still be as confused and unfeeling as before. Or our feelings can be a camouflage. Anger can be hiding hurt; tears can be hiding rage. A constant smile can be a kind of manipulating hostility or a mask for shyness. An aggressive, pushy personality can be a cover-up for fear. But once we begin to feel our feelings, to know what they truly are, our life begins to change. Our thoughts can lie to us; our body, our feelings tell us the truth infallibly.

Few of us had a perfect home or childhood. We were not touched or hugged enough, we were not listened to or praised enough, we were pushed or made to feel guilty, and very likely we were manipulated by someone else's needs. Some people live in the past and spend a lifetime feeling sorry for themselves because of a troubled childhood. Then they reinstill the same pattern in the children entrusted to them. We can blame a third-grade nun for our bitterness toward religion and our fear of sex. We can tell victim stories for hours about our parochial education and the attendant trauma. If knowing the reasons could have healed us, we would long ago have been cured.

Search offers us a chance to forget the past and deal with any present bitterness or fear. Years of ineffective therapy may have only made some of us conscious of how deprived and wounded we were. We have cried enough about the past, cursed it, pitied ourselves, and blamed all of our present problems on past misfortunes. The extensive misuse of therapy has taught us a new idiom to explain away our personal deformities, but it has not helped us to feel better about ourselves. *Search* can teach us to grow up and take responsibility for our present feelings, to get rid of the ghosts. We are not sick or mentally ill. We do our work and take care of our responsibilities. But we have to confront our feelings of bitterness and fear, not continue to offer sophisticated reasons for our condition.

A STEP TOWARD FREEDOM

For relatively healthy, functioning people *Search* is an important step to joy and freedom. Such people may not have the taste or money for prolonged therapy; one can grow old with an analyst, or broke. One can also understand personal behavior according to a complex and beautiful theory without real growth or relief from anxiety and depression. To interpret human behavior with some theory or other can be a well organized guessing game. Some hurting individuals seek therapy although they don't need it because they don't know what else to do. *Search* can be of help.

In the course of my own struggle for self-acceptance and personal growth, I tried a variety of workshops from New York to California, at outstanding centers like Esalen in Big Sur, California, or in private homes. Some of them added to my self-understanding and my capacity to feel, but frequently the more dramatic they were, the less I really gained from them. At times I met a gentle woman who was a temporary answer to my loneliness, or I received enough hugs and compliments to feel good about myself for several days. But usually the fervor did not last unless I somehow learned to get in touch with my own feelings. Often I had sex with a woman when I wanted friendship, or I chattered and boasted when I wanted to cry or remain silent. When the group was gone and the excitement had subsided, I was left with my own resources in the undramatic framework of my daily life. I had no plan, no real direction, and my joy was short-lived.

Search does not guarantee an emotional explosion. It is a low-key, somewhat didactic program that provides principles that must be continually applied until they are absorbed into our basic consciousness. *Search* principles must be reviewed and practiced like a golf swing, not merely in the safe environment of the home or in a workshop, but in the context of real life.

In many workshops I was almost bullied into feeling. Or I was exposed to such warm, open people that little was demanded on my part. It was not hard to "bare my guts" if such was the desired effect of the program. Often my sexual feelings got in the way of my sadness or fear, or I manipulated the group like I had manipulated life. I received a temporary balm like an inspiring talk or sermon but gained nothing to instill self-acceptance and personal growth. I was entertained, "loved," encouraged to "open up," or to "let go," but I wasn't really taught much of anything. It was like learning French by drinking cognac.

Search does not force anyone to feel or to adopt the "party line." It does not demand information that a participant chooses not to share. The effect may not occur immediately, but it is long-range and lasting. It puts the burden of growth on the individual by announcing simply: "Accept your feelings without editing. Your feelings are you!"

AXIOMS:

- Listen to your body.
- Your feelings are you!
- Tension is blocked feeling.
- Play the long game!

Little boy I miss you with your sudden smile and your ignorance
  of pain.
You walked in life and devoured it—without anything
  but misty goals to keep you company.
Your heart beat mightily when you chased frogs and captured one
  too big for a single hand.
You wandered with friends in quiet woods and were startled
  by a shuffling porcupine.
Matches were a mystery that lighted fires and chewed up leaves
  in savage hunger.
There was no time for meaning—a marshmallow gave it
  on a sharpened stick.
A jackknife in your pocket provided comfort when your friends
  were gone,
A flower in the woods hidden by an aging, shriveled log,
A dog who danced and licked at your fingers or chewed your jeans,
A game of football you didn't expect, a glass of cider, a cricket's cry.
When did you lose your eyes and ears, when did taste buds
  cease to tremble?
Whence this sullenness, this mounting fear, this quarrel with life
  demanding meaning?
The maddening search is leisure's bonus—the pain
  that forbids you be a boy!

From There Are Men Too Gentle to Live Among Wolves

2. The Fragile Balance Between Dependence and Independence

Principle Two: *As you begin to feel, recognize the dependencies in your life and take responsibility for your own happiness.*

THE BLAMING GAME

For many years I blamed the Catholic Church for ruining my life. I was loathe to realize that my fear and dependency, my actual addiction to the Church, was responsible for my unhappiness. Theoretically I could have left the seminary any time I wanted. Actually I was bound there by my own feelings of powerlessness and weakness. I didn't have the strength or support to leave. So it took me ten years in the seminary and ten years in the priesthood before I was able to make a responsible decision.

I could spend the rest of my life blaming the pope or my bishop for my unhappiness. Or I could blame myself. Either would be a destructive and pointless action. What happened, happened. I wanted to be loved and to feel valuable, and I chose the course that was available to me for my own survival. The important thing is that I recognized the fear and dependency that were making me emotionally sick and did something about it. Of course, the Church did not make it easy. When I left in 1967, there was only guilt instilled in anyone who challenged ecclesiastical authority. When I visited my bishop in Lansing, Michigan, he was kind but firm. I could not leave. He offered me a small parish in the southern part of the state where, with minimal duties, I could write and reflect. I declined. He accused me of being impatient. I told him I had only one life to live and I had to get on with it. He said I had made a commitment and that all the changes I wanted, new attitudes toward sex and birth control, divorce and law, would occur. I told him I had already changed, and with his reluctant permission I left in my Volkswagen with everything I owned stashed in the back seat. I felt wonderful, but my odyssey had only begun.

Ultimately, to the Church my unhappiness didn't matter. If I were unhappy, it was due to some moral fault of mine. I did not believe this. Gradually my anger grew more intense. My understanding of what the Church had been in my life became more enlightened. I realized that my Church had been largely a home for uneducated immigrants like my own forebears and that it had bound its members with fear and guilt and ignorance. For some in a once hostile, biased America it was probably a great and important institution; for me it was debilitating and crippling. Yet I had known this a long time before I left.

FEAR AS DEPENDENCY

Why did I not leave sooner? I feared the wrath of my family and friends. I feared that I would not be able to make a living. I feared loneliness and my own lack of real experience. Curiously, I did not fear God. I had settled matters with him. But I hung on to get my Ph.D. even though I knew that I had serious differences with the Church. I had become a priest against my own desires. I wanted to please my family and the priests who loved me. I did not know that I had to please myself if I were ever going to be happy. My dependency was destroying me and I was not even aware of its existence. I cannot tell you how frightened I was to make the break—and this after twenty years of service. I just hadn't seen any way out.

The year before I left I was visiting my brother Phil, a psychiatrist in California. He was working in a therapy group with a few priests from the diocese of San Diego. He invited me to join them. Up until this time, I had engaged in a variety of fantasies about leaving the priesthood and I was even able to experience a modest degree of sexual fantasy without great guilt, but

I still had been unable to foresee how I might leave the priesthood. I was the small, frightened boy of fifteen who feared to disappoint his pastor and his mother. The therapy group was amazing. These priests talked like human beings. One had been dating a woman regularly and had decided to marry her. Another felt that he was a homosexual. Two more had made up their minds to leave the priesthood. I couldn't believe my ears. No priests I knew had ever talked like this.

At the time I was a priest-student at the Catholic University of America when there were a hundred of us in the same residence hall taking a variety of disciplines to earn our various doctorates. There were liberals and conservatives, eggheads and plodders, sinners and saints, the pompous and the down-to-earth. I was friends with a number of them, but no one I knew talked about leaving the priesthood. They questioned the Church's stand on birth control, divorce, celibacy, mortal sin, hell—you name it—but it was taken for granted that the priesthood was forever. Suddenly in San Diego, a huge weight seemed to fall from my shoulders. It seemed that all I needed was to hear a few priests talk about their vocation as if it were not chiseled in stone. I had been released from the intellectual moorings of the Church for some time; only the emotional dependency, the fierce addiction remained.

FREEDOM IN STAGES

I remember clearly a few hours later skipping like a kid along the beach screaming at the top of my lungs, "God! I'm free! I don't have to be a priest!" But even when I confronted the bishop and left a year later, I took a leave of absence to soften the blow, to let my parents and friends think that I might be coming back. Sometimes we are not strong enough to leap off the cliff; we have to climb down the mountain a step at a time. But we have to start climbing. Deep in my consciousness I was quite certain I would never come back, but I was still too dependent to make a clean break. With all due respect to myself, I did it the way I had to. I was a frightened, quasi-adolescent who had given his life away to please others and I had paid dearly for it. And leaving the priesthood was only the beginning. I had made a move to save my life, but my dependency had become a way of life.

When I wrote the book *A Modern Priest Looks at His Outdated Church* I was an instant celebrity. I was again dependent, this time on the attention I received. But, as I would write years later, the "triumph" didn't get the job done:

It is no triumph to be admired
Like a mountain peak or a pine forest . . .
Admiration knows nothing of dawn's tears
And the gathered fears of a confused lifetime.
Nor is it any solace when a brother is dying
And life is trying to make a mockery of all I've become.
Cowards and braggarts are as admired as brave men,
Liars and charlatans are as esteemed as the truly honorable,
    Because admiration sees but the surface
And is lulled by the spell of one's own imaginings.
Tonight it is enough to be admired by no one,
To rest in your arms and to know that you love me enough
    To read the dim corners of my eyes,
    To hear the pauses on my lips,
    To rest together in a silence
Where there is nothing to admire—and everything to love.
                    From *Maybe If I Loved You More*

LOOKING INSIDE

Admiration was empty. It was its own addiction. I had to go further and to discover myself, to find within my own heart and soul what my life was meant to be. I had looked outside myself, listened to the projections of others, wanted to please as I had been taught, found God's will in what others told me. Now I had to look inside.

There is quiet water in the center of your soul,
Where a son or daughter can be taught what no man knows.

There's a fragrant garden in the center of your soul,
Where the weak can harden and a narrow mind can grow.
There's a rolling river in the center of your soul,
An eternal giver with a rich and endless flow . . .
So remain with me then, to pursue another goal,
And to find your freedom in the center of your soul.

From *There Are Men Too Gentle to Live Among Wolves*

The dependent person looks outside for relief. He or she can be addicted, for example, to a romantic version of love.

Roger, a swarthy, talkative, lively, and charming man of forty had dated endlessly and slept with a variety of women. Curiously, he had a dim view of all women: they wanted a "free ride"; they "had no morals or loyalty"; they only wanted "to control a man and take him over." Yet he still continued to search, neurotically frequenting dances and bars, singles' clubs and idyllic vacation spots with Club Med or on cruise ships. It was always the same story. There was an initial excitement, a chance to tell his story again, a brief affair, and an ensuing depression—and no personal growth. He did not know how to make a friend; he had become addicted to novelty and sex. Even the sex grew tiresome because there was no caring or spiritual sharing in his varied relationships, yet his whole preoccupation was with more women; he had practically no real male friends. He was as addicted to sexual excitement as he might have been to cocaine or alcohol. And like any person with an addiction, he was not free. He did little to develop his own capacity for happiness. He was convinced that he would ultimately find the right woman and all of his loneliness would go away. His dependency was destroying him and he feared he was an alcoholic.

Again, *Search* did not offer him a cure, but he began to have some insight into what he was doing. He began to feel his insecurity and depression, his acute loneliness and anxiety. He saw that after a while he did not really make contact with women even while he dated them. When the sexual excitement was gone, they did not remain friends. He just moved on, looking for another conquest. He never considered his preoccupation an addiction. When on rare occasions he went out with a male friend, his whole focus was any women around. He reminded me of a poem I wrote, "Drinking with an Old Buddy":

So how long's it been, a year?
Whatta you been up to?
(Did you see the lungs on that one?)
You had a breakdown? Just couldn't pull it together?
Man, I feel for you! (Look at the ass on that one in red!)
Out of work for six months? Unbelievable pressure!
    No one to talk to?
(Oh, man, I'm in love! Get a load of that body!)
Why didn't you let me know? What's a buddy for?
(Christ I'd kill for a night with that brunette.)
I still can't understand why you didn't call me!
    What's a buddy for?

From *Maybe If I Loved You More*

CUTTING THE CORD

In one sense we all learn dependency in childhood, but a *Searcher* seeks to replace dependency on parents and take responsibility for his or her own life. Our goal is to recognize the dependencies we have in our adult lives and decide whether they help us grow according to our deepest feelings or not. There is often great pain when a relationship ends and we sometimes, for the very first time, become responsible for our own happiness. To recognize a dependency is to make a decision about it.

Mary Ellen, who looked like a pretty blonde teenager, was in an unhappy twelve-year-old marriage, but she feared to be on her own. It would have been chaos to have simply jumped out of the relationship. She had no job, she had responsibility for two children, and she was financially dependent on her husband for everything. She was his "little girl." Her high-pitched, whiny voice and childish demeanor reflected it. For years she had simply fantasized about other relationships. Then she had a brief affair with an Episcopal priest, which introduced her to the first exciting sex she had ever known—in the back seat of a car at the end of a deserted cul-de-sac. But the priest was happy with his marriage and Mary Ellen was just a diversion to him. For a long time she hated him for it, but feared to confront him; she wasted her positive energy devising schemes to get even with him, or longing for the right man to come walking into her life. Her first step was to recognize the fact that she was dependent, trapped and imprisoned in an unhappy relationship; the second step was deciding to do something about it.

She thought about getting a job, about self-improvement, about joining a women's support group. Gradually her whole outlook changed. She stopped playing the blaming game and began to do something about her life. She did not have to attack her parents for allowing her to grow up without discipline or attack her husband for neglecting her. She might even find a different kind of marriage if she began to overcome her addiction. It was not a miraculous cure, an instantaneous solution. *Search* seldom is. For five or six years after the marriage had soured, Mary Ellen did nothing. Now she had direction.

IMPACT OF DEATH

Sometimes the death of a loved one can precipitate an unending depression. It did for Carol, a sad-faced, buxom, and handsome woman of fifty-four. She could not get over her husband's death. She had been terribly dependent on him; she did not even drive a car and a checkbook was a great mystery. Long after the time for healthy grieving had passed, she had fallen into a severe depression and received medical help. The depression began to lift when she recognized and decided to do something about her dependency. Later she wrote me that she was going to teach school again as she had twenty-five years before. There was no self-pity in her letter. She was reading, attending an aerobics class, and had joined the Church of Religious Science, which had introduced her to new friends and excitement. She was beginning to take charge of her own life.

Many of us are thrown back upon ourselves through a ruptured relationship, a job loss, or poor health. The child in us begs for someone to take the pain away. It is healthy to be aware of the child that lives within us. It is wholesome to let the playful child out from time to time, to learn to laugh and frolic and let go. But the dependent child can be a killer.

INTERDEPENDENCY

This is not to say that everyone has to be free of all dependencies. A solid friendship or committed love is an *interdependency* wherein we meet one another's needs. That's what life is all about. Total independence can be a mask for one who fears any dependence and intimacy. We need each other. We need to reach out, to share the burden of living, to find the helping hand when we are lost and alone. One of the most important things I learn in my contact with *Searchers* is that people want to help us if we are willing to stand on our own feet. No one wants to be around the "drainer," the consistent "whiner," the perennial child who wants to turn everyone into a parent.

CONTROL AS DEPENDENCY

Even the dominant person in a relationship is ultimately dependent. Jerry, tall and rigid and athletic, was a kind of petty tyrant in his marriage. He wanted to know where his attractive wife was at all times. He called home constantly when he was on the road because he feared she might be seeing someone else. He decided where they would go, how they would live, whom they would see. But in tying his wife so tightly to himself, he was also tied to her. He really had no more freedom than she did. In giving his wife the freedom she needed to grow, he gave freedom to himself, but he had never before recognized his controlling behavior as a form of dependence.

ADDICTIONS

Our dependence on addictions can take the form of any

number of things that only seem to make us happy but leave us emptier than before. Possessions, status, money, financial security, prestige, health, sex, and activity can be as addicting as drugs and alcohol. St. John of the Cross once said wisely that it doesn't matter if a bird is bound by a chain or a silver thread, it is still bound. Cultural pressure can also bind us contrary to our own most profound desires.

Virginia, a pretty, apple-cheeked, motherly-type woman admitted to me that she liked waiting on a man, but her female support group attacked her for her behavior, so she resisted doing thoughtful acts of service she really wanted to do. Then she discovered that she did not have to be brainwashed by the group; she could be the person she wanted to be. She was attracted to the strong, confident male and found great joy in pleasing him. Her dependency on conforming exactly to the prescriptions of her women's lib group could have destroyed her own personality.

NEED FOR AWARENESS

There is nothing wrong with a dependency, or better yet, an interdependency, as long as we are aware of what is taking place in our lives. If our personality is fulfilled, if we feel honestly like ourselves, we do not need to listen to the accepted and current behavioral system that seems to be in vogue.

Phil, a balding, thin, gentle stockbroker, was uncomfortable in his relationship with Sally. Sally was so preoccupied with her job that she had no time to talk about anything else. He wanted to travel, to spend leisurely weekends wandering without plans. He liked movies, conversation, two- or three-hour dinners, books, and skiing. But there was never time. When he argued the point, Sally accused him of being old-fashioned, jealous, afraid of competition, of not wanting a "real woman." None of these accusations seemed to fit and he began to realize he was entitled to the kind of relationship he wanted, the "new woman" notwithstanding. So he knew he had to move on despite the pain. Changing Sally was impossible and was not his place. She had the right to be who she was: intense, work-oriented, upwardly mobile. And Phil could assuredly find someone else who met his needs.

FEELING TRAPPED

So many people feel trapped because they fear to take the initiative and free themselves from a job they hate or a relationship that cripples and depresses them. They feel guilty about seeking what they want from life. *Search* urges us to play the "long game," to take one step at a time, and to monitor our behavior. We don't have to run right out and quit the job or leave the relationship. Perhaps that will be the final result, but the important thing is to recognize dependency and to decide if it is destructive. It helps us personally to look to the God within, or the life force within, and try to remain in touch with our own dreams, but as long as we are addicted to anything or anyone, we will never be free.

It takes courage to escape an addiction. It may take counseling or therapy for a time. Assuredly it will cause pain, but the pain will not kill us. It is a kind of death and resurrection experience and we will rise to a new level of life. We are doomed to unhappiness only if we choose to be.

One of the exercises I use effectively in the *Search Workshop* is to pair people up facing each other and direct them to turn the palms of their hands toward one another. At first I request that they do not touch. I ask one to lead and the other to follow; then they are asked to alternate. After a while I tell them to touch hands. One is told to become dependent, to let go, and to follow the other. Then they are asked to reverse the process. Finally, I insist that they both attempt to lead. Usually this brings chaos, but at times the pair is able to achieve a kind of rhythm whereby neither is conscious of real leadership. This is a visual example of true interdependence, the veritable rhythmic relationship mature individuals seem to be able to achieve in their friendship. This exercise is an interesting one for couples to try on their own and often creates intense and surprising feelings.

It does not take much reflection to realize how dependent we are on many things in life: the air, our food, transportation, housing, job, neighborhood, dentist, doctor, lawyer, friends, even our local bartender. The person who needs nothing or no one is seldom attractive; neither is the person who desperately needs something or someone. It is in balance that beauty and freedom emerge.

AXIOMS:

• Interdependence allows you to live fully without losing your personal creativity and identity.

• Extreme independence is often the mask that dependency and fear of intimacy wear.

• Dependence is healthy when you take responsibility for your own happiness.

• Play the long game!

It's time to clothe my dreams in reality,
To move beyond jealousy and possession,
    isolation and imprisonment,
To confront boredom and loneliness, sadness and lovelessness,
To make known my secret needs and reveal my hidden yearnings,
To risk self-exposure as the only path to final freedom,
To surround myself with the energy flowing from the earth's core,
The passion of rivers and resilience of trees,
And thus, to clothe my dreams in reality!

3. The Importance of Meeting Our Own Needs

Principle Three: Make an assessment of your own needs. Decide what needs are not being met. Do not edit your needs. What they are, they are.

THE DISCIPLINED LIFE

I often think of the hours and days, the months and years I spent in the seminary denying myself the things I wanted most. My whole life seemed to be discipline—parsing Greek and Latin verbs, rushing from one exercise to another, struggling with my relationship with God, meditating and praying and eating on schedule, ignoring my most basic desires for love and freedom. And all to please someone else, to gain a love I never really got, or a love I could have had anyway if I had resisted all my fears and guilts. I remember the occasional moments when I admitted to myself how miserable I was. But I had no right to be miserable. God had called me. That was all there was to it. So I returned to the chapel, gazed sadly at the crucifix for hours, and said, "Thy will be done," not realizing that the God who spoke through my feelings was more real and direct than the crucifix.

It wasn't that I didn't like to learn; I did. But this wasn't really learning. Learning is a passion, an interest, a preoccupation with satisfying an innate curiosity. This was a competition, a Herculean labor, an attempt to prove that I was as bright or brighter than anyone else. My intellectual tastes became jaded, as if I had eaten the wrong food for a very long time. I was reading about saints when I wanted to read about adventurers. Even the *Iliad* and *Odyssey*, which we studied in Greek, or Vergil's *Aenead* and Livy's story of Hannibal crossing the Alps into Italy

35

were not literature; they were Greek and Latin games, attacked sentence by sentence. I never identified with the courage of Hannibal or the anguish of Achilles or the power of Agamemnon. It was all a scholastic game. Years later I wrote about my education and the myopia and denial in seminary life.

Once a lad with untold eagerness for love and life
And questions in his eyes for which there were no words,
With energy like bubbling springs emerging from the ground,
Made his way to silent groves in academe and found
A grammarian's gravity to tell of Caesar and Homer in words
Without surprise, dim and dull, replete with rules,
Insisting that Achilles was but a genitive attending "heel"
And Agamemnon proper subject of a sentence scarcely real.
The blood was parsed from books, poetry lost in ponderous prose,
Reading but a rat's performance memorized by those
Who fought for little pellets of A's or B's
And heard grave warnings made to boys who felt the breeze
Of Troy or made of Hannibal a hero on his elephants
When masters bade him trudge across snowy Alps,
Only to lead a verb again in search of its object.

The lad became a kind of man
Replete with scholar's expertise that seemed to promise love
But offered testimonials instead, and left him filled
With anguish and emptiness, disgust for learning,
A seething desire to hang a collection of his masters
Until the blood flowed from their infinitives and tenses
And their flesh could modify the ground
    In search of all their senses.

Stupid lad! You should have known! A single glance enough:
Gray buildings with bilious yellow halls—no music calls
Or flowers, only Spartan sundries, clean terrazzo floors
That only seemed like stone, but tasted lean
    Like disinfectant and cement.
Barren bathrooms, waxen toilet paper, beds aligned like coffins,
Windows without curtains like prying eyes, the air dead,
Food, pale and pasty, a desperate creation,
Where potatoes disappeared in some milky, motherless creation . . .

And oh, the sallow cheeks that checked his every move,
Making it tense and angular till nothing round survived.

Circles made no sense amid triangular and esoteric gods.
But most of all a lad who wanted love, a reason to laugh,
And got instead a scholar's rules and daily duels
To break a spirit till he cried, "I will not die!"
But tried so hard and such momentum built to stay alive
That even now he struggles badly to survive . . .

From *Will You Be My Friend?*

NEEDS AND PERSONAL IDENTITY

It was an education not unlike that of thousands of others who considered discipline the secret of all of life. To pursue one's own needs or to follow one's own inner light was self-indulgent and sinful. Now I understand that God or our personal deity speaks to us through our needs. If we are to recognize ourselves, if we are to have some sense of our own identity, it is our personal needs that tell us who we are. The psychologist Abraham Maslow has spoken tellingly of the hierarchy of needs, insisting that if our basic needs are not met, we will never ascend to the higher ones.

MY CELIBACY

And celibacy itself had no meaning for me; it was a mere deprivation. I liked women; I loved their company—the dimension they added to my life, their warmth and insights, their ability to make me feel worthwhile and loved. But if I was going to be a priest, even at fifteen I was to avoid all personal contact with women, regardless of my personal needs. I was so starved for feminine affection that merely to brush my hand against that of the beautiful young nun who helped us do the dishes was a tremendous erotic experience. I would plan my moves at the dishwasher with proper awkwardness so that this experience occurred several times. I think she enjoyed it as much as I did. At least her eyes told me she did.

The result of all this was the manufacture of an efficient, bright, controlled individual who would spend years trying to get in touch with his own feelings and ultimately to discover his own needs. And yet, I do not now blame either the program or the men in charge. They had inherited a cultural system they promised to uphold. Some of them sensed it was madness but had little choice but to leave. Now, some thirty years later the whole Catholic Church is in a state of chaos. Pope John Paul II still attempts to impose the system he inherited. Meanwhile the people drift away unless they are too frightened to leave or mature enough to make their own decisions. Many do not know that God speaks in another way, through one's own heart and spirit. But *Searchers* do not get fixated on the past. What's done can gradually be undone. Once we are in touch with our feelings, we can again get in touch with our most basic needs and forgive the individuals who were as much victims as we were.

DENIAL OF NEEDS

I was certainly not an anomaly of some sort because I studied to become a priest. Thousands of married people deny their physical, emotional, and spiritual needs and try in vain to find some species of happiness. It is interesting for *Searchers* to spend time by themselves making an actual list of needs that are not being met. Writing them down seems productive. It helps to begin with our most persistent needs and discover that getting in touch with our unedited feelings assists us in discovering our unmet needs. Needs can be ignored or suppressed for years, until we no longer feel the possibility or the right to have them met.

A DEPRESSED SPOUSE

Doris, a sad-faced, almost mousy woman of forty, had lived for five years with a severely depressed husband, an accountant, who felt unable to work and refused medical or psychiatric help. He spent most of his time in bed, at times watching TV or reading, but usually brooding morbidly over his acute pain. Doris worked every day to support a family of four, but she had become a virtual prisoner the rest of the time, attending to his needs and refusing to go anywhere if he chose not to go. Finally, upon advice, she began gradually to pay attention to her own needs; she visited friends, attended movies and workshops, and gently refused to remain at home brooding with her husband. Over several months, with great effort and courage, he began to do things with her and struggled heroically to go back to work. Finally he was able to seek help, was prescribed suitable antidepressants, and their life became relatively normal. Had she refused to meet her own needs, the marriage would likely have ended or her husband would have been a prime candidate for permanent disability or suicide.

THE MARRIAGE ILLUSION

Marriage so very often means an end to individuality. Fortunately much has been written on this subject lately. How often men give up their buddies once they are married and couples go everywhere together—or nowhere. They get in a kind of a rut where it seems easier to stay at home and watch TV than to continue to be the active, involved persons they were in single life. So many couples presume that all of their personal needs will be met in the marriage relationships.

Bernie, a stocky, bushy-haired machinist, discovered after six years of marriage that he was totally bored with his life. He had given up fishing and hunting and a twice-a-month poker game and spent his weekends taking care of a yard he actually hated. The only way out seemed to be a divorce. His wife, Cheryl, with the face of a movie star and a figure to match, was no happier. Their sex life had fallen apart, her time was spent exclusively with the kids, and Bernie had become the weekend gardener and game watcher. Football, baseball, basketball, even hockey, which he barely understood, filled in the time between crabgrass and gopher holes.

When they made a list of their personal needs, they were startled at the vast numbers that were unmet. Bernie wanted male companionship, hunting trips, good sex, weekend travel, private space in the house, a sense of being valuable to his wife, and ultimately his own business. Cheryl was unaware of most of this. The whole idea of a potential divorce startled her, especially since they were devout Catholics. She had no idea what had gone wrong. When she listed her own needs, she mentioned leisurely talking and touching, time away from the kids, movies and plays she wanted to see, some religious or spiritual contact, some appreciation for her work, and a degree of financial independence. Marriage had made them both dull and resentful, each blaming the other for needs that were not met.

Of course, recognizing unmet needs does not automatically get them met, but it is an important start. Bernie had ceased to know who Cheryl really was; nor did she know him. After a few years of no real communication, they were mere color patterns and familiar, unheard sounds. They did not even argue; they just privately brooded and believed that life would mean more when the kids were grown. *Search* offered them an important alternative. None of their needs were unreasonable; none of them could not be met. The last I heard, Cheryl had taken a job and loved it and Bernie had taken up fishing again and made contact with college friends. Their marriage was more secure since the lines of communication and need had been opened.

Very often, as we know, all of our needs are not met in our primary relationship. Yet, the media bombardment in our culture leads us to believe that they should be. I sometimes think that romantic commercials are among the most destructive forms of relational balderdash. Numerous couples who strive valiantly to look good on the outside, as if their relationship is ideal, are actually lonely and miserable. They somehow are willing to suffer, to offer an attractive appearance to the rest of the world. Often I study their body language and their eyes and know that all is not as it appears.

TAKING RESPONSIBILITY

Change takes place when *Searchers* begin to take responsibility to meet their own needs, to take the risk of being the persons they really are. This is frightening. They fear it may mean an end to a relationship when it is in reality the only chance they have to begin it. No one can really know our needs unless we express them. And no one is consistently going to meet our needs except ourselves. Many of us are angry because a spouse or friend does not guess what we want. Or we lose sight of our needs for years, as I did, and play an elaborate masquerade. Few people knew how lonely and depressed I was as a priest. I just kept busy, kept smiling, and only in the privacy of my room or car did I give in to the feelings of sadness. More often, I created elaborate fantasies that never came to pass.

I denied my sexual needs until they erupted dramatically. I lived docilely with somewhat tyrannical superiors for years until I exploded. At one I threw a bowling bag filled with the seat collection money. Later, another invaded my office when I was chatting with two young women; I grabbed him by the collar and threatened to punch his lights out. I was branded as dangerous and explosive, and I probably was. Actually, I was ignoring my needs until my whole being revolted and overreacted. I survived by keeping busy and by spending as much time as I could by myself. I was still the little boy wandering in the woods, afraid to admit to others who he really was. Even now, I am sometimes that same boy, still suppressing my own needs to be thoughtful and "nice"—and miserable.

ALCOHOLISM AND NEEDS

Veronica, an overweight fifty-year-old woman, drank away her needs once the children were raised and her husband remained absorbed in his work. Alcoholics Anonymous helped her to stop drinking and offered her a solid program to transform her life. *Search* helped her understand her personal needs. She wrote out a two-page list, a fact that startled her. Her whole self-worth had been tied to motherhood. She was afraid to get a job, afraid to make friends independently of her husband, afraid to go back to school, afraid to indulge her talent in art. She felt poorly educated and uninformed, as if she had nothing to offer anyone. Her husband talked about his work and international affairs, quoting *Time Magazine* or the *Wall Street Journal*. Her whole personality had been subservient to his. Because he did not appreciate music or theater, good literature or travel, she had not allowed herself those things; she simply dissolved in his shadow. Thus her needs were absorbed in alcohol or erupted in an intermittent ulcer. When she got in touch with her own feelings, she became aware of her needs and began to look years younger. She stopped blaming her husband and got on with her life. Ultimately they were divorced.

At times the mountains seem insurmountable now
As I gaze at them from the safety of a warm, flowering meadow.
There is snow upon the peaks and chill winds gust angrily above me.
Yet, as safe as the meadow is, I have been here too long,
And the song of the birds has grown dull,
The flowers seem artificial and the frogs too content.
I want to fly myself above the peaks, sing my own songs,
And climb till every vestige of every dream is silent.
Why am I afraid to travel where my own destiny draws me?
Why do I hesitate when a familiar echo, deep in the caverns
    of my Heart calls me?
There is no time to reminisce, to watch the circling crows
    and drifting clouds.
It is time to move lest winter harden my limbs and freeze
    my most sacred needs and dreams.
It is time to move boldly and bravely and to remember
That the purest air is waiting in the heights,
And a single step is enough to be on my way.

GOD SPEAKS THROUGH NEEDS

So often we expect a miracle or remain lost in those fantasies that dull our minds and clog our movements. We are impatient, or all seems so vast and hopeless that we hesitate to take the first step. For this reason, *Search* continually talks about the "long game," about imagining our life a year or five years from now. It will be no different then than it is now, if we do not take responsibility to meet our own needs. God or an inner spirit speaks to us through our needs. It is our own private revelation. We do not need a guru, and for that reason *Search* does not offer one. When I lead a group, I am struggling along with everyone else in it. Each of us is our own priest, our own shaman, our own guru.

THE PLEASER

Vince is an athletic, vivacious man who has had little success with women. Three marriages and numerous relationships have all ended. In his early forties, he is nice looking, is a successful attorney, has a brilliant and curious mind, and enjoys multiple hobbies and interests. He loves travel, skiing, the ballet, tennis, professional sports, and is a decent gourmet cook who loves to entertain. He is an outstanding host and an exceptional listener. Lately he has wanted to give up on finding any enduring relationship. Friends fix him up with blind dates, his job puts him in touch with a variety of divorced women, but nothing ever seems to work out. He has grown increasingly unsure of himself and tries too hard to please.

When he began to become aware of his real needs, he was able to admit that he wasn't himself with women, although he prepared elaborate meals, took them to posh restaurants, planned interesting trips, listened to their problems, and was always gracious even when they stood him up at the last minute. He blamed himself when women turned him down or didn't respond to his calls. It became clear that the women sensed his mask, as well fashioned as it was, and were ultimately turned off. He compared himself unfavorably to a bachelor friend who gets along with women extremely well and doesn't have "as much to offer" as he did.

"They wait on him, invite him to dinner, do what he wants,

defer in almost anything, try to please him. I'm always on the other end of the stick, but it never occurs to me until I look back over a relationship or marriage. I realize I've given expensive gifts, given up football games for an opera or a stupid family reunion, deferred about vacations or the house we lived in, agreed to go out for dinner when I want to stay home. In retrospect, I get angry as hell! And I feel sorry for myself because I've been taken advantage of. I wish to hell I could be a more demanding, aggressive, son-of-a-bitch!"

Vince could wish to become more aggressive or he could become aware of his own needs. To be a son-of-a-bitch would be another facade. Once *Search* helped Vince become aware of his own needs, he began to be himself without playing "nice boy" or "macho man." He began to be the beautiful person he was without searching his past to discover why he was still trying to please his mother. If he learned what he wanted and began to ask for it, he would be real, not a mannequin of accommodation. It all begins with needs, his needs. And if he spent a lifetime ignoring them, he would end up alone or acutely lonely.

It is hard to focus on our needs when we have been raised with an artificial understanding of unselfishness. Vince really was manipulating women, giving to them with the expectation it would all come back. When it didn't, he was furious. Later he told me that he had arranged his needs in a kind of hierarchical list and was systematically setting out to realize them. He had even met a woman, he told me laughingly, who found him too demanding. He was beginning to learn that he has the right to have his needs met, needs that are at the core of his very existence, perhaps his closest contact with God.

AXIOMS:

- Know your personal and professional needs that are not being met.

- Arrange your needs according to their priority and begin working on them.

• Take responsibility for your own needs.

• Play the long game!

The only sanity left is madness, madness enough to resist
  all that is respectable and decent.
I stand among the lonely at their luaus and cocktails,
Hear the stories I've heard before, study the strong men's faces
  and see the dullness of their eyes,
Endure the silent pain of docile and obedient wives.
I watch niceness replace passion and fear give birth
  to sterile kindness.
What is there left to be proud of?
  A yard without weeds?
  A car without scratches?
What remains to boast of?
  Money in the bank?
  A computer that finally tells you how to live?
Sometimes I wish life were a deck of cards
That had to be reshuffled every few years.
  Blacks would be married to whites,
  Salesmen would be nuclear physicists,
  Astronauts would be chimney sweeps
  And chimney sweeps would be surgeons.
  Poets would be bartenders and lawyers poets,
  Skinny women would be fat and fat women men.
  Old men would be boys, and young women
    would be frightened matrons.
All at the turn of a card, the shuffle of a deck,
And life would be wild and crazy and alive again.

PERSONAL FREEDOM

I cannot answer for all the others
Nor understand their uncomplaining compliance
With routine's demands and painful boredom.
I know little of age or settling down,
Or boundaries established by history and custom.
Grey hair is no barrier or wrinkles,
Time spent or time remaining means nothing
To a heart that requires freedom to live.

In another life I carried my tent across the desert,
And sailed my creaking ship across an unknown sea.
Now I wander freeways and crevices, hear unknown voices,
And make friends with whomever is at hand.
This is not a choice I made, but a destiny I inherited,
Not a habit but a freedom of blood and bone and madness.

Stand back from life and observe it at a distance.
What makes sense and what is imprisonment?
Who knows consistent freedom and who follows a path
Made by ants following ants in prescribed procession?
I have no idea where I must live or how,
No blueprint made in Japan or heaven,
Only a heart and mind that know what is true and false,
And what it is to feel the pulse of freedom,
Without which, for me, there is only a premature death.

4. Beyond Dreams and Illusions to Options

Principle Four: *Decide what your options are and select the options best suited to meet your needs.*

Once we become acutely aware of our needs, it is imperative that we find out what real choices and alternatives we have. None of us are omnipotent. We have heard a thousand times from eloquent after-dinner speakers that we can do anything that we set our minds to. I am not convinced of that.

A close friend of mine, a therapist, has always wanted to be a writer. He has tried off and on for years to write an account of the kind of work he does and the significant experiences he has had. He is one of the best counselors I know. I learn something every time I talk to him. He has worked with drug addicts, in prisons, and in racially sensitive areas; he is charming and handsome and an eloquent conversationalist. His practice is eminently successful and his clients are lavish in their praise. He is a born therapist, but for him even writing a paragraph is torment. For years he asked my help, struggled on his own, and felt depressed and discouraged because he couldn't get it all down in print the way it really was. Finally, wisely, he gave up and has dedicated himself to his practice. Only rarely does he talk of writing and then smiles benignly, with resignation.

A few years after I left the priesthood, I started a business to refinish, for insurance companies, furniture that had been damaged by water or fire. I got the idea when I had an extensive fire in my beloved Victorian home in San Francisco and discovered that the repair work was not being done well. People were running all over the place making bids and removing chairs and carpets. It was a mess and I was livid. I threw them all out and arranged to do the work myself. Gradually I expanded my service to cover anything in the home that was classified under a fire insurance policy as "contents." It was a great idea and a financially rewarding one. I had abundant energy for about a year. Then I realized that my writing was suffering, that I did not have the temperament to argue with housewives about what was fire damage and what was normal wear and tear. Late one night, when an angry matron called me at home to complain endlessly, I exploded and suggested that she have the man-in-the-moon and Humpty Dumpty do her work. I decided that if I were to do something other than write and lecture, it could not be repairing furniture for picky housewives. I knew I needed to do something other than write, but this complicated, tense, picayune business, even though financially satisfying, was not for me. It was no longer a real option.

OPTIONS AND NEEDS

Options are related to needs, but, then, so are fantasies. The difference is that fantasy can be a way of avoidance.

Denise, a forty-year-old attractive divorced brunette, eagerly wanted a good relationship with a man, but she did nothing productive about it. She fell in love with movie stars, wrote to celebrities and expected them to call, read romantic novels, and occasionally had a drink at a corner bar. As a secretary in a small office, she seldom met anyone except the Xerox service man; she even began fantasizing about him although he was married and had five kids. Fantasies seldom consider what is possible, although at times they can be the seed of a dream and ultimately the root of an option. For Denise, fantasies added nothing to her personal growth and ultimate happiness. Gradually recognizing the game she was playing, she joined the Sierra Club and went on real outings with real people. Her correspondence with the stars came to an abrupt ending.

I am not discrediting fantasies. Some of my happiest moments have been spent in indulging them. I thought of the novels I would write, the movies that would be done from my work. There probably would be a part in one of the films for me and I would be discovered as a late-blooming Marlon Brando. My fantasies got me through a painful day or night, but they did not succeed in meeting my more pressing needs.

Terrance, a popular minister with wavy hair and a charismatic personality, admitted at *Search* that he wanted a divorce for years but feared that it would end his religious career. So he spent those years fantasizing about women in the parish or plotting ways to have a successful affair. He became listless at home, bored and restless, and wasted untold energy in attempting to fantasize his way out of an unhappy life. He had never even talked honestly to his wife about his feelings. This was his first option.

He didn't attack or accuse her. She was a vivacious, religious women who loved her faith and was proud to be a minister's wife. Even though they had not had sex for two years, she didn't seem to miss it. Terrance expressed himself honestly and they agreed on a trial separation. Later they were divorced and he was sent to a smaller parish in the northern part of the state where he loved his freedom and his work. The last I heard, his wife was engaged to another minister. Terrance had let five or six years slip away because he was afraid to talk honestly when it was his only real option.

OPTIONS ARE NOT PERFECT

Unlike fantasies, options are seldom perfect. You can't drown your children or inherit a million dollars. *Searchers* learn to select the best option available to meet their needs. If we hate our home, we can move. If we despise our job, we may gradually take steps to find another one before giving up the one we have.

Katherine, a thirty-year-old Catholic, had married when she was eighteen and pregnant. She was never really in love until she met an attractive bachelor who was coaching her son's soccer team. For the first time in her life, after ten years of marriage, she realized that she had made a mistake. Her experience with the coach merely made her recognize that she still had a lot of living to do. She wanted to leave her husband, but she had no real skills in the job market. So, the first thing Katherine decided to do was to make plans for her departure. She felt that bursting impulsively out of the marriage would have left her with minimal support and perhaps too much stress to achieve her goal. So she stayed in the unhappy, but not miserable, marriage for two more years until she had a good job and a secure future. She would have liked to leave the marriage much earlier but she decided it was not a viable option.

Ted, an artist, wanted out of his marriage for a long time but felt guilty about it even though his wife was self-supporting. His guilt revolved around the fact that she had supported him for almost three years. She was madly in love with him, he said, and dissolved in tears and rage every time he talked about a separation; she always dragged up the hard work she did and sacrifices she made on his behalf. Even to leave for a weekend to attend an art show really upset her. He fantasized for a long time about what it would be like to be single, to be able to devote more time to his work, to travel and thus to broaden his outlook, to study other works and meet exciting people in his field. All of this seemed impossible in his marriage. After he got home and had dinner, he either went out with his wife or he stayed home with her and watched TV programs he hated. Or he entertained people he didn't enjoy. After a *Search Workshop* he took the first step in the direction he wanted to move. He called to say he wouldn't be home for dinner and managed to survive. Later he spent the night in his studio three or four times a month. It was a beginning and he was taking the option that was possible for him, given his guilt and fear. Perhaps some solid therapy will be necessary ultimately to move him along in the direction he wants to go, but acting out in the face of guilt is a good beginning, and often a cure.

Options have to do with the quality of relationships, lifestyles, finances, children, parents—any phase of our life. The important thing is to reduce our ruminations to practical reality, even if things don't turn out exactly the way we want.

Sometimes an individual's options have their comic aspect. I wrote this poem about a friend of mine in Canada who was going through a mid-life crisis. I found out later, when I went through my own, that there is nothing funny about a mid-life crisis, but I still enjoy the poem, and, given a little poetic license, it is almost historically accurate.

According to psychological surveys, John is in a mid-life crisis.
He left Gert, his wife of twenty-six years, as a relic of a previous life
And married a *Playboy* centerfold, sans stretch marks
    or thigh bumps,
A beauty named Debbie—aren't they all—whose teeth shine
    like the flesh of a MacIntosh apple,
Whose breasts are the two sipping fawns of Solomon's love poems,
And whose skin is so creamy John gives her welts
    with his drying forearms.
At first the mid-life crisis was only feeling silly in a custom
    T-shirt with "Daddy digs mama's pears" in four colors
And too tight jeans that made his testicles turn blue.
Later he aggravated an old hernia at an all-night disco,
Ruined Debbie's first vaginal orgasm with a burst of emphysema.
. . . On a camping trip around the Mediterranean, he developed
    arthritis, pellagra, skin lice, and was robbed in Turkey.
Although he attended rock and jazz concerts, EST, bought a wok,
    and learned to read tarot cards,
There was nothing to talk about and he sought psychic help
    when he compulsively had a Buddha tattooed around his navel.
After three visits to an holistic healer Debbie used to live with,
They all began sleeping together in a giant waterbed,
Dined on rice and steamed vegetables and traded mantras
    once a month.
When John did not improve he called Gert to return for a weekend.
After four martinis, pig hocks, sauerkraut, and a Dutch Master,
    John finally felt free enough to break air.
. . . The next day he watched three football games with a six-pack
    while Gert prepared his favorite foods and did the dishes.

He told her how great it was to be back and slept soundly
on an orthopedic mattress.
After a sausage omelette and four cups of coffee, John uncapped
a beer and settled down to watch two more games.
Gert cleaned the kitchen and kissed him softly on the forehead.
Then she gave him the house keys and went off to live
with Debbie and the holistic healer.

From *Walk Easy on the Earth*

OPTION, NOT IMPULSE

When I speak of options, I am not talking about impulsive
behavior. *Search* is always concerned with the "long game." To
act on impulse is often the refusal to feel the feeling that may
well be at the very core of our option.

I am the world's greatest authority on this defect. So very
many times when I had a serious decision to make, for example, to end a relationship or to begin one, I would hop in my
four-wheel-drive vehicle and head for the hills. I was afraid to
face the deeper, more painful feeling that would lead to personal freedom. I simply kept moving so that I would not have to
experience what was really going on. When my brother Bob
died of cancer, the third brother in as many years, I cut short my
grieving and drove up and down the freeway like a crazy man. I
could not make up my mind where I wanted to live. Since he
was next to me in the family and we had been priests together,
our friendship was lifelong and beautifully intimate. He was
the one person I could go to at any time of the day or night
without the least fear of rejection. He was my roots, my port in
any storm, and his love for me was both apparent and abundant.

Of course I grieved during the three months I knew he was
dying. But when it was over, I could not face the depths of my
pain. If I wanted to let go of him, my only genuine option was to
let my tears and grief pour out no matter how long it took. Impulsively, I kept moving and tried to decide where to live. Of
course I could not make a decision because there was a more
vital matter that required my attention. Without him, I was not

really certain that I wanted to live at all. I was not prepared for his death. I am quite certain that my own demise could not be more acute. My impulsive behavior, however, was totally ineffective and only succeeded in making me depressed and sick. Until I could somehow accept his death, release all of my anger and pain, I was not really free to get on with my life.

Some impulsive behavior, however, is just an expression of the thrill of living—a sudden decision to jump in a plane and head for San Francisco, or a swim in the ocean at two in the morning, or, as I once did, a drive to Mexico on the way to a movie. At times these impulsive actions are amongs life's greatest gifts, but not when the impulsive behavior is a refusal to deal with what's really going on.

OPTIONS AND AGE

For many people age becomes the deterrent; we do not have the option to begin again because we are too old. But this is not true. A therapist friend of mine finally had a happy marriage after five tries and twelve grandchildren. Another friend of mine went back to law school at somewhere around fifty-five. I remember when I was twenty-three I decided I didn't really want to be a priest. I visited a counselor at Kalamazoo College in my home town and asked about the value of my seminary credits. A cryptic, insentive man, he had no perception of my fear and confusion. I had already completed college with a B.A. in philosophy and had finished three years in theology. I wanted to know how long it would take to become a psychologist. He gave me all of three minutes and told me that it would take at least six or seven years since my credits were worthless. It did not matter that he was totally in error. I was crushed. Six or seven years would mean that I would be thirty before I got to work. And, of course, that was "too old."

When I was seven I told my mother I was too old
   for short pants, and when I was in fifth grade,
I quit wearing knickers. Too old again.

When I was twenty-three it seemed too late to start over
in a new kind of work
Because I hated to waste two extra years of college.
So instead I spent ten years
Working at what I didn't want to do, changing my way at thirty-five
When I was too old at twenty-three.
Yesterday I thought I was too old not to be settled
and successful and thought maybe
I'd get in some kind of work that might make me happier
and have a promising future.
I called my best friend and asked his advice.
"Aren't you getting a little old for that?"

From *Maybe If I Loved You More*

CHANGE AND GROWTH

Change is usually a painful process, but it is the raw material of growth, and options are the practical blueprints of change. It is always important to ask ourselves what is possible for us. We may not be able to leap off the cliff like someone else. It took me five years to leave the priesthood after I knew I wanted to. It took a friend of mine sixteen years to get out of marriage after she realized it was over. No matter. We are who and what we are. The essential thing is that we move at our own pace to create our dream, as long as we still have the courage to dream. There are so many changes I still have to make, so many miles I still have to travel. I have spent so much of my life trying to please others rather than to do what I really wanted, and in the end I was pleasing no one. Fear and guilt hold many of us back for whatever reason. If we remain concious of our needs, write them down, review them frequently in the order of their importance, and select the options best suited to fulfill them, we will move step by step toward the creation of our own life. Brooding and fantasy just won't get the job done. Pursuing options will!

Perfectionism is a vicious and destructive kind of fantasy. It ensures that we will never be satisfied. Competition works the same way. Perhaps, like me, you were somehow pushed to be number one in whatever you attempted. I was expected to be valedictorian, to make the varsity team, to master whatever I undertook, and to prove that I was better than anyone else. Whatever the genesis of this disease, it caused me to live with a variety of unfortunate illusions. When I wrote poetry, I expected to reach the heights of Walt Whitman or Robert Frost; I measured my novels against Steinbeck and Faulkner, even though I knew I was an entirely different person.

With such a competitive outlook, I couldn't enjoy what I was doing. When I finally recognized that I wrote the way I wrote, with my own pluses and minuses, I no longer had to be anyone else. Now when the reviewer attacks, I can realize that the opinion expressed is only that of the reviewer. Thus increasingly I make it a point not to read reviews, and not to compare my writing to that of anyone else. If I live with illusions about my own ability, I will never be satisfied. If everything I write has to be perfect, I will write nothing. Gradually I recognize that some people enjoy what I write and others don't. They are no different than I am. I don't particularly like F. Scott Fitzgerald or Faulkner, and I doubt very much that they would pore over every word that I write. If I can view my own work realistically, recognize that my option is to be me, then I can be satisfied with what I do. I can also accept the kind words of others about my work and not be defeated when I don't make a best-seller list. I want to enjoy what I do, to let it flow freely and rhythmically and to know that it is mine. If I live with illusions, I will never be satisfied. Overcoming perfectionism has been a constant struggle for me, but gradually, through reprogramming my mind, I am winning the battle against illusions. Alas, I'll never be Shakespeare! But then, Shakespeare will never be me. (He probably never hit a winning backhand down the line.)

AXIOMS:

- Relate needs and options; establish a hierarchy for each.

- Reduce fantasies to real, practical options.

- Visualize frequently and in detail the life you want to create.

- Play the long game!

I want to walk with you above the pines,
Scale mountains, leap rivers, speak to the sun and moon,
and make wagers with the stars.
I want to roll laughing down lonely canyons,
To tease the desert that threatens to destroy,
ski deserted trails,
Ride dirt bikes to the very edge of the lingering horizon.
I want to sail across strange seas and explore buried cities,
To watch the mating of whales in a Mexican lagoon,
And hear the music of coyotes across a moonless sky.
I want to startle deer in forests and mountain lions
in their lairs . . .
But most of all I want to love without barriers,
With eyes laughing and hearts singing
And caution abandoned to the clouds by a friendly west wind.
I want to feel your presence as my very own, to speak to you
As though I am talking to myself,
To hold you without fear or distance or private thoughts,
So I can walk with you above the pines, scale mountains,
leap rivers,
And make wagers with the stars.

From *Laughing Down Lonely Canyons*

5. The Power of Decision Making

Principle Five: *Make decisions and abide by them. Indecision is the prime destroyer of living energy.*

Several times in my life I have made myself ill by my inability to make decisions. On such occasions I reviewed my various options endlessly and was afraid to act on them. I guess it happens to the best of us. I remember the psychologist Rollo May asserting that he stayed in a marriage for nine years because he feared the loneliness that would ensue if he left it. I have no doubt that every day he reviewed his worn tape of the situation and sought the comfortable way out. At least that's what I have always done. And the stress remained until I finally made a decision.

In attempting to leave the priesthood, I rethought my position hundreds of times before I was prepared to make a decision. I flirted with compromising situations, fantasized every possibility, but I was afraid to make a final decision. On vacations in Florida or on trips to Lake Michigan, I would meet attractive women, usually say nothing or lie about my job, and come as close to intimacy as my conscience would allow. Then I would return to the priesthood, still painfully lonely in the life, afraid, convinced I wanted to do something else and tired of a pointless celibacy. I remember driving from Flint to Grand Rapids, Michigan, and wandering around by myself without the distinctive Roman collar that set me apart. I had to get away, yet I did not know what to do with myself. For a few hours it was exciting to be alone. Then I grew restless.

I walked the streets, ate dinner by myself, and finally I decided to go to a movie. A young usherette led me to my seat with a flashlight. There was hardly anyone in the theatre and I invited her to sit down next to me. After a few dull frames of the picture, I realized I was too restless to sit still. I suggested that we leave and go some place else. She said she would be free in a half hour. Suddenly I was excited and alive. She was a beautiful young woman and I was startled that she agreed to go with me. I presume she was lonely as I was.

We drove to the sand dunes of Lake Michigan, sipped a little wine, and talked far into the night. There was a strong chemistry between us and ultimately we began kissing and fondling. She was the most attractive young woman I had ever held in my arms. I still remember her exquisite face and the perfect contours of her body. We touched and explored and only stopped short of making love. It must have been three in the morning when we finally left and I drove her home. At a dangerous intersection, I barely avoided a head-on collision that would have killed us both. Suddenly I felt guilty and afraid. It was as if God were speaking to me in screeching tires and smoking brakes. I took her home and never saw her again.

But I thought about her frequently. I wanted to spend more time with her, to get to know her, even to leave the priesthood with all its demands and artificial roles. Instead, I returned to the rectory, confessed my "sin" and continued to masquerade as a happy priest. At times I could lose myself in my work, punish myself for straying by working even harder. Then the loneliness and meaninglessness of it all engulfed me, and I began wandering again.

I fantasized about leaving the priesthood, fantasized about making love with the beautiful woman of the sand dunes, but I continued to live the predictable life that increasingly made less sense to me. I was paralyzed and could make no decision. I could not accept the priesthood and the Church as it was, nor could I be honest with myself and take my leave. The young woman was frequently at the rim of my consciousness when I taught class or even when I said Mass.

Often I fantasized about other women in the parish or even the high-school and college girls I taught. When I preached my sermons or taught my classes, I was totally conscious of the loving eyes that seemed to stare at me. They made the lectures and homilies exciting. It is not that I really ignored everyone else. As a priest I made a sincere effort to prepare my sermons carefully and preach the gospel as I understood it. But once in the pulpit or in the classroom, I could on many occasions feel my adrenalin rise as I indulged my fantasies and dreamed my way out of the priesthood. Of course, nothing really changed. I only took more chances and began to live on the fringe of my vocation.

Sometimes when my work was finished in the evening, I would wander to a town some distance away, change my clothes in the car, and sip a beer at a favorite bar where I knew that unattached women gathered. It felt good to be another human being and not a priest. Most often I spent the evening alone or in dull conversation. At times I danced, necked in the parking lot, then felt guilty and confessed my "sins." With new determination I tried to live the total life of a priest, but the dreams and fantasies seemed stronger than I was. I prayed, read more books, worked harder, and tried to associate more consistently with other priests. All of this worked for a time and then once again I would wander off in search of some vague freedom, longing for the softness and understanding of a woman.

DREAMING OR DECIDING

Looking back, I was no different than an unhappily married man. In fact, after I left the priesthood, when my marriage was not working, I did much the same thing, only then it was more likely to include sex. I continued to dream my way out of the situation, stayed in the relationship out of guilt and fear, and continued to be confused about who I was or what I wanted. When I finally was able to divorce, I found that I could live more comfortably alone and I did not have to lie anymore. Life wasn't perfect, but at least I did not have to sneak around like an awkward gigolo. I had made a decision and now I had options that were possible. But for years I had moved in circles, afraid to get in or out of the priesthood, afraid to get in or out of married life. Marriage didn't seem to work for me. So if I dated a woman several times and it seemed that she was already planning our dream house and organizing my time, I would usually end the relationship and begin again. Alone.

FEAR OF DECISIONS

But most of all I frequently found it impossible to make the necessary decisions. Brief alliances with women were never ultimately satisfactory since I had no real life plan and consistently gave double messages: "I want you and I don't want you." I presumed the perfect woman would stumble into my life, solve all my needs, and I would be happy forever. I knew better in reality, but my fantasies, unlike my true options, were always perfect. Even in beginning relationships, I found myself unable to make clear decisions and abide by them, especially if the woman was persistent and determined to wrest from me some sort of fragile commitment. I created my own fantasies about how my life would be, kept others at a distance, and frequently feared making decisions or implementing them. I was the traditional passive male, and no matter how many relationships I entered into, they were doomed because I did not really know what I wanted. Or if I knew I didn't express it. Or if I expressed it, I would somehow find myself working hard to be loved and then giving in to a programmed courtship that I had verbally and eloquently rejected a few weeks before. So instead of making decisions, I ran away and started again.

When I did enter into a significant relationship, I acted again like I did in marriage or the priesthood. If I felt pressured, instead of making a decision to talk about what I was feeling, I usually began to hedge in communication, even to lie, so that I could preserve some semblance of my own identity without terminating the relationship. The stress would build and the tape would start to play in my head, sapping my energy with the drain of indecision.

DECISIONS AND PERSONAL PROGRESS

Gradually I have become more decisive and more capable of being myself, but it has taken such a long time to achieve this kind of sovereignty. My progress has been proportionate to my ability to make decisions and to abide by them. When I couldn't make decisions or tell the truth, I suffered intensely. The last few years of my priesthood were a constant turmoil. I knew it was all wrong but I feared the consequences of my potential decision. If I were to leave, my family and friends would be upset, God would be angry, and I would soon be broke and unemployed. I smoked more, drank more, worried more, pondered more, and created more elaborate fantasies even as I stayed on the job. Thus, my energy was constantly drained.

I was not unlike Eleanor, a teacher and mother of three children, who spent eleven years dreaming her way out of her marriage. She had a few brief affairs at conventions, had a painful, ongoing relationship with an insensitive bachelor who taught at another school, and finally ended up in a breakdown. She had exhausted herself in refusing to make a decision about her marriage. And she made no improvement until she took a positive step and decided to get a divorce—eleven years later. The prolonged indecision and unsatisfying duplicity destroyed her positive energy, and she only came alive when she faced the reality of her life situation and made a decision. Meanwhile she had wasted years fantasizing her way out of an unsatisfying life. At *Search*, she admitted that she had taken what men came along because, while she was still in her marriage, she had no freedom to relate to someone she could truly care about.

PAIN OF INDECISION

There was a time when divorce seemed impossible and to leave the Catholic priesthood was a disgrace and perhaps tantamount to eternal damnation. But even now, when society is more tolerant of such changes, millions of men and women live in the misery of indecision and do nothing but fantasize about what could be.

Terry, a shy redhead with a great sense of humor, hated her job and dreamed of a hundred other possibilities but took no action. She, too, was afraid to make a decision. After much personal effort, she finally began taking the necessary steps to do something else with her life. She had lost so much self-respect in her job and was so burned out from attempting to meet unrealistic marketing deadlines that she had no sense of her own power. She lived for the weekends when she could smoke dope, listen to music, and dream her troubles away. She talked of writing a novel, of owning her own business, of meeting a rich man who would take care of her. Religiously she read the job ads in the newspaper and the relationship ads in a singles' magazine, but she never answered any. *Search* helped her to play the "long game," and to begin step by step to make decisions and to create a life that reflected her own identity. As long as she was content to dream and drown in indecision, there was no need to take action.

GUILT AND FEAR

Decisions are not easy. As I look back on my life, I can add up the seemingly wasted years and feel very depressed about my vacillating behavior. So can Terry and Eleanor and hundreds I have met. But this only increases our evaporating sense of self-worth. For most of us, significant decisions take time and we do the best we can. Guilt and fear stand in the way. As a marriage counselor, I realized that I didn't really do too much counseling. I frequently felt like a hired gun. One party wanted out of the marriage but could not make the decision to leave. I was paid to provide freedom for the unhappy party, who was seemingly unable to escape under his or her own power. Many couples talk their dying relationship to death and hope that God, magic, or their partner will make the decision for them.

Neal, a construction worker, admitted to me that after years of indecision about his marriage, he used to fantasize about his wife's death in an automobile accident. When they went on a vacation to the ocean, he thought she might possibly drown. He stayed in his marriage for fourteen years even though he knew it was over at the end of the third year. In the meantime he developed an ulcer and emphysema. His body had made a decision years before, but Neal could not implement it.

MENTAL HEALTH AND INDECISION

Mental hospitals are filled with people who fell apart rather than make a decision. Many of us in unsatisfying relationships torment ourselves, deny our feelings, run away, keep busy, dream and fantasize, have affairs in reality or in our heads, and continue to go on as if some angel of mercy will finally appear to save us.

Irene talked about her bad relationship for ten years to anyone who would listen. Finally everyone was tired of hearing her, even her therapist. She was admitted to the psychiatric ward of a West Coast hospital and three weeks after her release committed suicide. She died rather than make a painful decision that was destroying her.

I am not making a plea for divorce. I am making a plea for honesty and courageous decisions, which are the raw material of change and growth. We spend so much of our lives pleasing others to win their love that we lose our very identity in the process. To make a decision for our own health and happiness seems selfish and even sinful. Our sense of responsibility extends in every direction except toward ourselves. Actually, we have made the decision in our own secret consciousness, but we are afraid to act on it. We are trapped in our own "goodness," which ultimately destroys us.

Larry spent fourteen years trying to please his mother,
And nine years struggling to please his father.
He spent four years rushing to please his boss,

Ten years wanting to please his wife,
And twenty-six years determined to please his kids.
I thought the preacher summed it up well.
He said that Larry lived a pleasing life.

From *Walk Easy on the Earth*

A PROCESS OF CHANGE

Search is not a magic formula. It merely gets profoundly practical and urges that we initiate the *process* of taking action. Perhaps most of us cannot make a giant decision all at once. We fear leaving a job lest we be without income. We are terrified of the loneliness following divorce and the horror of playing the single's game. But we can begin the *process of change* by making what decisions we can. Perhaps it is a sufficient start to admit our unhappiness, or to decide to prepare ourselves for the future. We cannot continue to live with destructive indecision. The stress will only build up and destroy us.

DEALING WITH INDECISION

When I was trying to make a decision to leave the priesthood and could only replay the same tired LP in my mind, I did what I could to make the final decision less painful. I began to amass the necessary credentials to be a child and family counselor before I left. That way I was prepared at least to make a living. Even when paralyzed by strangling indecision, we can decide to make new friends, to shore up our support system, to go back to school, to get a part-time job if we have never worked before, to take one day a week alone to reflect positively on what decisions we need to make to improve our life. We can decide to communicate honestly no matter the cost, to begin to be who we are to the extent that we can. There is no deadline, no rule of thumb that covers everyone. Many of us have been taught so intensively to think of others that it takes us years to respond to ourselves. We are so attuned to someone else's pain that we ignore our own. To make *any* decision, to take *any* positive step is vastly preferable to wrapping ourselves in self-pity and pointless fantasies that never lead anywhere or simply to suffocate in indecision.

ANGER AS AN ALLY

Often it helps to get in touch with the anger and even rage that we have buried in our present state of existence. It is far less costly than getting in touch with anxiety and depression or mental illness. Anger can be a source of energy and more than once it has helped to save a life. I remember almost being drowned in a rip-tide off the coast of Mexico and I became so enraged about dying in such a stupid, pointless way that I was able to summon up new energy and save my life. When we have been put down enough or have suffered enough personal degradation, our anger can be an important ally to rescue us. Often we forget that anger is a powerful part of our emotional makeup and it can save us from self-annihilation. When summoned, anger often enables us to respect who we are and becomes a significant source of self-love.

Once your eyes rested on me like a child, helpless to turn away.
Now they drift into shadows or beg to be amused
    like a restless puppy.
Is security the ultimate oath that love will never be?
Is contrived gentleness the only currency in circulation?
I like raging men, unreasonable men, outrageous men,
Who know a love the feeble and frightened never understand.
I am no manservant, no prisoner chained by contracts,
No serf who pays gentle homage and receives his supper in return.
I have always dreamed of love bordering on madness,
Not settled instead in decency and logic.
A curse on decency that strives to control what it cannot love,
And only loves what it cannot control.
Mothers still insisting that their little boys comb their hair,
    And put the peanut butter jar back into the cupboard,
Like altar boys, keeping all the rules, or boy scouts
    masquerading as men.

Lust asking permission, rage taking out a permit,
  Lest it lose what it never had.

From *Laughing Down Lonely Canyons*

BAD DECISIONS

Making a decision does not mean that we cannot later change our minds. Even a bad decision is more constructive than languishing in endless indecision. It helps to clarify who we are and what we want. It can be a positive source of new energy.

Ron, a thirty-eight-year-old salesman, separated from his wife of eleven years, feeling, as he put it, that he was only a "check book" and a vacation planner. No one in the family really cared what he felt. His sex life was dull and unimaginative. When he brought home some erotic movies to play on VHS, his wife considered him an incipient pervert. He left the marriage, got his own place, and after initial pain and loneliness, felt good about it. After several months he and his wife were able to communicate on a new level. They began "dating" and gradually discovered a new bond of love, but it was the decision to leave that was the real catalyst of change.

DECISIONS AND NEEDS

Decisions are directly related to our unmet needs and options. If we are conscious of our needs and seek practical ways to meet them, the decision gets the job done. It is interesting to note how many men in *Search* are starved for close male companionship.

Doug, an architect, noted that he had friends with whom he occasionally played tennis or racquetball and business associates with whom he had lunch, but the special camaraderie of college and premarriage days was gone. For a long time after his marriage, he was content to spend time with his wife or to do things with other couples. When he began to feel a certain loneliness, he recognized that he had abandoned all of his male friendships. His wife seemed to be on a more intimate basis with her friends. Doug felt a need to talk about something besides business and sports. He finally admitted that he had not a single close male friend. He reacted strongly to a poem I read to a group of *Searchers*.

Women gather
    Free to chat of impotent husbands and not quite forgotten lovers,
    Sharing dreams with old or new friends and confiding desperation,
    Baring souls and unburdening hearts, then leave
        relaxed and laughing,
    Promising to lunch again soon, freed from the pain
        of no one knowing.

Men gather
    Free to boast of the money they've made or will make soon
        —or the women,
    Displaying how strong and controlled they are
        and unafraid of competition,
    Sharing triumphs and hiding themselves, then leave
        with a handshake and "See you around,"
    Bleeding silently within themselves, bearing the pain
        of no one knowing.

From *Maybe If I Loved You More*

DECISION PRACTICE

Usually in *Search*, I divide the participants into groups of three or four and ask each person to spend five minutes talking about a decision he or she is in the process of making. This is a good exercise for couples at home as well. Since I am not interested in theoretical decisions, I again carefully point out that a decision should relate to unmet needs and be a practical way of reducing fantasies to genuine options. If individuals are clear on their needs and can arrange them in some sort of hierarchy, then it is usually a simple matter to know what decision is crying to be made. If the decision cannot be made all at once, some part of it can, and thus *Searchers* are always in the process of making a decision. Or they recognize that they are not yet ready to make a decision. As Fritz Perls, the famed Gestalt therapist, once wrote, "I have decided not to decide." This positive attitude prevents us from wallowing in the debilitating stress of indecision.

Sometimes individuals are startled at the decisions they make. Or they may have to admit that they have been struggling with a decision for many years and have not acted upon it. At least they begin to recognize the connection between decision and growth, and the tragedy of so many lives wasted in fear and unhappiness because a decision cannot be made.

Shortly after leaving the priesthood, I worked with an experienced counselor whom we nicknamed "the fastest short-term therapist in the West." His whole method was to assist people in making decisions. Often on a Monday morning, when each of us ushered a new client into our respective offices, I was still serving coffee when I heard screams of protest coming from his office. A man or woman had come in to complain about a marriage and Bill said simply, "Why don't you break up?"

The startled client went on to say that there were some good things about the relationship. Bill then suggested, "Stick it out! Why expect any more?" Then he sat there and said nothing while the person protested loudly that he or she had paid for a full hour. Bill usually suggested gin rummy or an Irish duet, or he offered to read an interesting article he recently discovered. His whole method was based on making decisions and he never lacked clients. Whenever I had a problem to resolve, he was always the one I sought out. His expression would change from friend to counselor and it didn't take any ten sessions to get down to the nub of my problem. Hardly twenty minutes. I knew what I had to do; I simply was afraid to make a decision. He was the one who taught me that even bad decisions lead to action and growth. And I doubt he ever saw any client more than six times. Spending more time than that to make a decision just didn't make any sense to him.

THE DARK SIDE

It is often important to confront the "dark side" of a decision, to face the fears, even write them out, that prevent us from deciding. Then, at least, we can begin to recognize the blocks that lock us in a state of confusion. Many people have found that it truly helps to make clear to themselves the worst thing that can happen to them as a result of a decision. Whatever it takes, we must make decisions and abide by them. Our personal growth is at stake, and ultimately, our personal happiness.

AXIOMS:

- Prolonged indecision can lead to serious illness.

- Decisions follow from unmet needs and practical options.

- A bad decision is often better than no decision.

- Play the long game!

Yesterday afternoon I decided, decisively
    To build an orphanage on fifteen acres.
In the evening I planned my own commune
    Which would include plumbing and clean napkins.
This morning I knew I had to get married
    And have seven kids like my father.
An hour ago I determined to build a house with my own hands.
I wonder if that buxom girl in the granny dress
    Would love me if she got to know me, and help build the house.
I wish to hell I'd get my laundry done
    And fix the kitchen sink.

                From *Walk Easy on the Earth*

6. Testing Personal Values and Uncovering Guilt

Principle Six: *Examine your belief systems. Recognize the guilts that make you a prisoner of someone else's needs.*

Belief systems are collections of values and principles that underlie everything we do. They determine our attitude toward parenting, loving, being a man or woman, relating to God, working for ourselves or for someone else. They control our thoughts about money, pleasure, recreation, friendship, and success. They are at the core of every decision we make or seem unable to make. Our belief systems are inherited from our family and shaped by our environment and our culture. The struggle for personal freedom and integrity revolves around our effort to develop belief systems that are truly our own, ones that we can honestly live with. Someone has said that our belief systems are the silent assumptions we make every day, the truths we take for granted.

PARENTS

Brett, a gentle, successful banker, tried for years to make his mother happy. She could not support herself and had become his responsibility. He brought her to live with his family until his wife and children threatened to leave unless she did. She was in seven different rest homes and didn't like any of them. When Brett bought her a small, comfortable home of her own and engaged a full-time companion, she went through four roommates in a single year. He gave her whatever she wanted, but nothing seemed to satisfy her. When he visited her, he always came away exhausted and drained of energy. Her conversation was a litany of criticism of everyone in the family, of what she had done for them, of how little they cared about her, and of how she spent her whole life doing for others, all to no avail. Brett has two brothers and a sister who refuse to pay more than token homage to their mother because of her ever-present capacity to make everyone, even her grandchildren, feel miserable. Her alcoholic husband, who died a dozen years before, seems almost immortalized in her constant complaints about how badly he treated her.

Brett gave up his golf day for a Wednesday afternoon visit with his mother and denied himself clothes and vacations to buy things for her. He spent Sunday afternoons taking her for a drive, brought her gourmet food and fresh flowers, and then she complained about what he brought. Somehow, no matter what happened, he felt responsible for her condition, even though she had been unhappy all of her life.

With the help of *Search*, he began to examine his belief system about his duty to his mother and admitted that all of his efforts had accomplished nothing. With the shared help of other *Searchers*, he began to realize that he was neglecting his own right to happiness and the consistent depression he felt was of his own choice. Several months later, when he became far less attentive to his mother, he discovered that she complained less and was making an effort to develop friendships with people in the neighborhood. He began to realize that he couldn't make her over, that no amount of dedication would please her, and that her happiness was not his responsibility. He even began playing golf again.

Numerous emotional problems stem from a belief system that permits sensitive children to be manipulated by their parents. The guilt can perdure long after the parent has died, and more often than not little or nothing was accomplished by catering to an embittered, self-pitying, angry, totally self-centered parent. If we cannot be friends with our parents, perhaps only token homage is all we can give. An occasional visit, a card, some financial support may be what we can offer—but assuredly not our lives. Several times, *Searchers* have told me about having honest confrontations with their parents, surprisingly often to little or no avail. The common problem is that the parent, too, is operating from a faulty belief system, namely, that children owe their very lives to parents and should feel an obligation to help at any personal cost. Don admitted that he had not really liked his mother for many years and suffered most of his life because of her.

CHILDREN

The lives of many parents, as well, can be destroyed by a belief system that exaggerates their role in the lives of their children.

Deborah, an attractive, nervous divorced woman of thirty-eight, had lost all control of her teenaged son and felt that she had somehow failed him. His presence kept the home in a continual state of stress and confusion and may well have cost her her marriage. Every time she watched a TV show or read a story that revealed a good relationship between a mother and son, her guilt was only increased. She was afraid to date because she never knew when her son would be home or would create a disastrous scene. Her ex-husband refused to have anything to do with the boy and suggested that she contact the police when she was unable to curb her son's drinking and use of drugs. She had become a virtual prisoner in her own home. Her son took the car without asking, frequently skipped school, and was often gone for an entire weekend without her knowing where he was. Her belief system about motherhood demanded that she be a superwoman.

When the boy ended up in the drunk tank and then in juvenile hall, she was finally able to leave him there for two weeks. For a time, he seemed to improve. Then it was the same frightening story. When he began pushing her around physically, she finally sought professional help and ordered him out of the house. Over several months she began to recognize how her belief system about parenting had destroyed her life for several years.

SCREENING BELIEF SYSTEMS

No belief system should be beyond screening, especially when we feel overwhelmed in our personal life. I often encourage *Searchers* to take time privately to examine and then list carefully the belief systems that seem to cause them conflict. Sometimes it is profitable to trace the origin of our belief systems and discover that they are the gift of an overbearing parent or an archaic religion. *Search* teaches people to decide what is a real, personal value and what is simply inherited without appraisal.

Deborah's attitude toward discipline was part of her belief system; she had never been able to control her son. From the very beginning, his life had no boundaries, and when he reached adolescence, she had an uncontrollable monster on her hands. In reality, her son was as miserable as she was. She also admitted that she had stayed in her marriage eight or nine years longer than she wanted to because her religious belief system demanded that she stick out her commitment regardless of the personal cost.

RELIGION

Religion has destroyed countless lives with manmade dogmas that keep naive, sincere individuals prisoner.

Edna, a thin, pale woman in her late forties, had borne seven children in a totally impossible marriage. She was a victim of her childhood Church's position on birth control and the unbreakable bond of marriage. And her religious belief system never seemed to change despite what life and personal prayer had taught her. No matter what priest she talked to, the story was always the same. "God's will be done." And apparently God's will was leading her to a total breakdown. She grew to hate her husband but still believed that she had no choice but to stay with him. In recent years, after the Church began granting annulments even to long-term marriages, she felt angry and betrayed and stopped attending services regularly. When two of her daughters practiced birth control with permission of their pastor in the confessional, she felt that she had wasted her whole life. Most of her arguments with her husband, a truck driver, had centered around sex. When her belief system finally began to change, she felt that life had passed her by.

Another Catholic woman admitted to me that she lost interest in sex once her husband talked her into using the birth control pill. Her behavior had changed but her belief system remained intact. Gradually she was able to relate to the God who lived within her and to form her own faith. She liked the poem about *Elmo.*

Elmo prays, not because he's got the faith
  Or because he learned about God
    At his mother's knee or at a preacher's elbow.
Elmo prays because he tried everything else
  Drinking, screwing, running away, working,
To take away the pain of being a totally frightened man
  Which is totally unacceptable
    Especially to women and most men.
And none of this worked very well
  Till Elmo started talking to someone
    Somewhere, Who seemed to understand.
Now Elmo prays, not to Jesus or Buddha,
  Not to a theological God, or philosophical omnipotence
  Not to a computerized and selective savior.
Just to someone, somewhere, Who seems to understand,
  And loves the hell out of Elmo.

                   From *Maybe If I Loved You More*

I remember a crazy afternoon in Philadelphia when I was still the "Modern Priest Looking at His Outdated Church" and I visited a large department store to autograph books. There were two or three hundred people waiting in line. As I made my way to a podium, two elderly women attacked me. One ripped at my collar, and another clawed my face screaming, "You dirty Judas!" It happened too fast to frighten me, but later

I was able to understand their outrage. They had lived their entire lives under the rule of an intransigent Church that tolerated no exceptions to law. Now I was telling them that they could have ended a marriage or planned a family. It was too much to take. Their anger was not at me but at the pain and seeming folly of their own unreasonable belief system.

MY BELIEF SYSTEM

Like that of the ferocious women, my own religious belief system was formed early in life. It led me to the seminary and the priesthood without my genuine consent. I was the victim of my culture and feared that if I denied the vocation that everyone seemed to think I had, I would be destined to hell. I had heard enough stories at parish missions about young men and women who ignored their calling by God. Some were killed after an evening of petting in the back seat of a car, usually by an express train. Others later married and their children either drowned, burned in a house fire, or were born with scrambled brains. In such a belief system, God became a tyrannical ogre who got what he wanted. Even later on, in the priesthood, when I truly wanted to leave, I still feared that my soul would be damned eternally in hell, even though intellectually I questioned the very existence of such a place of torment. My rational mind and theological research were clashing with childhood emotions. A few years later, Pope Paul VI allowed priests to leave with some degree of dignity. Later, under Pope John Paul II, such respectable leave-taking became next to impossible. In a sense, I should be grateful for these papal contradictions since such obvious and confusing vacillations have given millions of individuals the right to form their own belief system. If the Church can change its mind, so can people.

But the "religious" horror remains because so many naive people are still trapped. An edict by the pope or a letter from the archbishop can tear their hearts out. In the belief systems of these untutored minds, God has spoken and all of their personal experience and awareness must be set aside. For this very reason, millions have left the Church of their childhood because they now recognize that the rigidity of religion is more an expression of history's rancor or a leader's bias than it is the voice of God. In my own struggle, for years after finally leaving the priesthood, it was impossible for me to enter a church or even to read the Bible or a religious periodical because I had been so poisoned by the belief system I inherited. Probably I went too far, but I had no choice. I was angry and hurt that I had been victimized by my own subculture. Years ago I wrote:

I left my traditions
   On the far side of a foggy hill.
And I will stay away
   Until I can return in sunshine,
      Rescued from them,
Free to choose
   Which are really mine.

                    From *Sunshine Days and Foggy Nights*

THE CONFESSIONAL

I can remember hearing confessions night after night of frightened adolescents who, filled with shame and remorse, admitted their numerous acts of masturbation and promised never to give in to temptation again. Of course they returned, experiencing over and over again the same shame and making the same futile promises until their obsession increased rather than diminished the number of their "sins." Finally, many grew strong and confident enough not to come at all. And who would blame them? I recall the courageous Paulist Father, now deceased, who admitted in a psychological work that masturbation was a normal part of adolescent development. The attacks from all sides were vicious and unforgiving, but he remains one of the early heroes who challenged the belief system of an archaic Church and freed thousands of people to live normal lives. Then he died by his own hand.

MARRIAGE

But it is not only religious belief systems that destroy lives with their wrathful attitudes about sex and marriage and sin. Almost daily I hear of individuals who remained in ten- or twenty-year marriages, because they believed divorce would damage the lives of their children or because they unfairly blamed themselves.

Recently, Cal, a quiet engineer, admitted to enduring a miserable marriage for nineteen years. Early on his wife had discovered he was having an affair when their own sex life had deteriorated, and he allowed himself to be punished for this misdeed in a caustic relationship with his wife until his early forties. He experienced an ulcer, a mild stroke, migraine headaches, and smoked three packs of cigarettes a day. His whole body screamed his unhappiness until he finally left the marriage under a barrage of criticism and began to live for the first time in twenty years. Looking back, he admitted that he couldn't really believe that he had bullied himself for most of his adult life. Such is the power of a belief system that denies the freedom a person's whole being is screaming for.

LIVING TOGETHER

The very words "love" and "marriage" are the products of a belief system. Togetherness and coupling can become a veritable prison for some individuals, or a new freedom. "Love" can be a practical, warm friendship or a romantic, impossible illusion. Marriage can be a sentence to boredom and depression or a living union in which two individuals retain the sovereignty of their own personalities. Living together instead of marrying does not necessarily change anything. There can be the same guilts, the same lack of honest communication, the same role playing and inescapable traps. Some give up on traditional relationships and create what works for them.

Steve, a balding, portly book salesman, after three unhappy marriages, has his own private apartment and is participating in a happy relationship two or three times a week and every other weekend. He and his friend often travel together and are comfortable with the kind of "marriage" they have created. They were able to let go of an inherited belief system that would have demanded a traditional marriage as a proof of love. I once wrote a poem about marriage and belief systems that is only half tongue-in-cheek.

Emma Burns is a martyr and stays with Jimmy
Only because she feels sorry for him,
Her folks like him, the neighbors expect it,
And he takes their two boys fishing every Saturday.
Emma survives by a furtive affair with Frank Harris
Every other Thursday afternoon.

Jimmy Burns is also a martyr and stays with Emma
Only because he feels sorry for her,
His boss likes her, the neighbors expect it,
And she is teaching the boys how to play the piano.
Jimmy survives by a furtive affair with Frank Harris' wife
Every other Wednesday morning.

The Burns boys are also martyrs,
They hate fishing but feel sorry for their father.
They also hate the piano but don't want
to hurt their mother's feelings.
They survive by smoking dope with the Harris kids.
Sin sure does have a way of keeping families together.

From *Walk Easy on the Earth*

FALSE BELIEF SYSTEMS

It is possible to spend a whole lifetime seemingly accepting a belief system that we actually reject. A man can achieve vast success at a job he hates because he adopts the cultural belief that his income is a measure of his worth. A woman who doesn't really want children can spend her whole life raising them, because she did not have the courage to resist her parents' belief system that holds that providing grandchildren is a duty. Her mother is delighted; she herself is severely depressed. Individuals live in neighborhoods that make them lonely because they think an expensive home proves their value. They may associate with a social group or belong to a tennis or golf club that they actually find boring or snobbish.

Delton and his wife have gone to Hawaii six times and the Caribbean four or five times to enjoy a much needed vacation. Delton admitted that he hated to lie on the beach and could hardly wait to end each "vacation" and get back to work. He usually grew restless after the first night, wished he hadn't come, and read worthless books to pass the time; or he drank until he fell asleep. He merely accepted the cultural brainwash that Hawaii and the Caribbean are veritable paradises. He loves duck hunting and long walks in the woods; he likes to explore ghost towns and has wanted to visit the areas where he fought in World War II. But in twenty years he never vacationed the way he wanted, because he accepted someone else's belief system about what is really relaxing.

Inherited beliefs enter into every facet of our existence and if we do not examine them, we pay a painful price. Millions of people become their victims.

"Women should cook and take care of the house."

"Men should be sexually aggressive."

"Children count as much as adults."

"Children should be seen and not heard."

"Homosexuality is the result of overbearing mothers."

"Christianity is the one, true religion."

"Hard work pays off."

"Neither a borrower nor a lender be."

HOMOSEXUALITY

Marlene told me that she and her husband had lost all contact with their son because he admitted he was a homosexual. Now that their belief system has changed and they are ready to accept him, they have no idea where he is. They bought the cultural prejudice against homosexuality and in the process were cut off from their beloved son.

EXAMINING BELIEF SYSTEMS

There are belief systems about dogs and cats, hunting and fishing, good manners and proper language, war and peace, nudity and obesity, wholesome living and social contact. None of them are wrong if they are really ours. When we find ourselves severely threatened by someone else's opinion or behavior, it is a good time to examine our own belief system and determine how solid it is. We do not have to agree with anyone else, but if we are comfortable with our own life and values, there is no reason to be upset by attitudes we cannot change. Even on sensitive matters like nuclear weapons and abortion, where opinions become volatile and even violent, it helps to know that our own serene conviction is more convincing than any amount of inflammatory rhetoric.

The tragedy is that individuals can spend a lifetime of unhappiness based on a belief system they do not really endorse. They amass money and then worry about investing it or outsmarting the IRS, losing the freedom they had when they were less affluent. Even trivial arguments can reveal a difference in belief systems. I remember one time using a four-letter word at a psychological conference and thus offending a devout, cultured woman. She wondered angrily why a man with my vocabulary and education had to use such a word. Was it a false picture of true manhood on my part or a sexual hang-up on her part? Actually, it was a clash of belief systems. I told her that I wouldn't analyze her opposition to the word if she promised not to analyze my need to say it. She smiled and agreed. But I found myself examining my own belief system and wondered if she questioned hers.

AGING

A person's ideas about aging can be a crippling belief system or a liberating one. Ageism is, perhaps, one of the most severe biases in our culture. If fifty or sixty or seventy is old and time for retirement, there are hundreds of people I know whose life became exciting and creative at just such a time. When passion and enthusiasm die, age becomes a factor, but not until then.

Hazel, a tall, rangy woman of seventy-two, refuses any senior citizen discounts and refuses to admit her age. "The minute I tell someone my age, I'm put into a category I don't want to be in. So I've been lying for years." She opened an art gallery of her own at sixty-three, travels to Africa and Australia, and is contemplating marriage. "Obviously, I'm too old to do any of that," she laughs. "I should be babysitting my grandkids."

BEAUTY

Men who are fanatic bodybuilders have bought into an elaborate belief system about masculinity. Women who spend hundreds of dollars and hundreds of hours on makeup have accepted a rigid, widely marketed belief system about feminine beauty. Our national preoccupation with dieting is a belief system that has become a growing obsession. The list of belief systems is endless and it is not my place to make a judgment about yours, nor you about mine. It is only important to understand our own belief systems and to decide if they represent who we really are or if they make us a prisoner of someone else.

AXIOMS:

- Know what your belief systems are.

- Challenge your own belief systems by hearing those of others.

- Abandon belief systems not in keeping with the person you really are.

- Play the long game!

Nothing has changed from childhood,
  The same longing for peace,
  The same hope for final fulfillment.

Life could have been easier had there been teachers
and wise men instead of drones imitating drones,
and parrots mimicking parrots.
If I were to begin again, I would challenge authority
from the crib, trust only smiles and laughter
that echo across all darkness . . .
Too many questions go unanswered.
Philosophers waste their time, even Augustine was
grave too soon.
I would have loved him before his conversion.
There is too much pain in the world,
Too much suffering without significance,
Till finally I know that love alone is worth the price.
Yet no one told me about love.
I was taught that conquests would fill the emptiness
beneath the surface of my heart.
Now I am content to be Aesop, selling my fables for
lunch money,
Satisfied to avoid black holes and galaxies,
Staying close to frogs and flowers and the smell
of baking bread.
. . . I woke this morning, wondering what was left to do,
Asking questions which only I can answer,
Finally grateful to love with a wounded heart.
So, for today, I will survive and for tomorrow,
Because nothing has changed from childhood,
Except I no longer permit anyone beyond myself,
To tell me what to do.

From *Laughing Down Lonely Canyons*

PERSONAL GROWTH

Somewhere along the way
A persistent voice taught me I was in competition
With every other man in the world.
I listened carefully
And learned the lesson well.
It was not enough
To find a loving wife and have average, happy kids,
To see a sunrise and wonder at an eclipsing moon,
To enjoy a meal and catch a trout in a silent,
    silver river,
To picnic in a meadow at the top of a mountain
Or ride horses along the rim of a hidden lake,
To laugh like a child at midnight
And to still wonder about the falling stars.
It was only enough
To be admired and powerful and to rush from
    one success to another,
To barely see faces or hear voices, to ignore beauty
    and to forget about music,
To reduce everything and everybody to a stereo
    color pattern on the way to some new triumph,
To rest in no victory, but to create new and more
    demanding goals even as I seem to succeed,
Until finally I was estranged and exhausted,
    victorious and joyless,
    successful and ready to abandon life.
Then somewhere along the way
I remembered the laugh of a child I once knew,
I saw a familiar boy wandering joyously in the woods,
I felt a heart pounding with excitement
    at the birth of a new day,
Until I was in competition with no one
    and life was clear again,
Somewhere along the way.

From *Maybe If I Loved You More*

7. Loneliness and The Building of a Personal Support System

Principle Seven: *Begin or continue to build a personal support system and sink new roots.*

LONELINESS

Personal loneliness seems to have grown almost in proportion to the progress and affluence that have evolved during my lifetime. For millions, the stable community, contact with family, the tie with Church, the struggle to make a living, the traditional values, the predictable neighborhood and familiar surroundings have changed. With new freedoms and multiple options there have emerged some unsettling fears and a deep insecurity in the lives of vast numbers of people. Few of us may be as trapped and bored as we were in the forties and fifties, but we have paid a great price in abandoning our safe structures and consistent traditions. And despite apparent progress, many of us, successful and uprooted, have isolated ourselves in our condominiums, our cars, our work, our thoughts and dreams, and even our leisure. It is as if a great many people really do not know how to live.

Loneliness can almost devour the sensitive and aware and cause a deep-rooted fear of abandonment and a diminished sense of self-worth. Others are able to keep busy, to anesthetize themselves with alcohol, television, sports, hobbies, sex, drugs, or whatever it takes to separate their minds and hearts from the painful reality of a lonely, stress-filled existence. Yet others simply sink within themselves and let life pass them by. They exist without really hoping for anything more. Even their dreams and illusions have gone dry.

Relationships that once lasted for a lifetime are often abruptly terminated, which results in hurt, often excruciating pain, and more loneliness. But at least as many fear the emptiness of divorce and separation and remain addictively in a silent togetherness that only adds to their loneliness. Even Rollo May, the eminent psychologist, admitted that his book *Love and Will* "resulted from nine years of struggle, knowing that I had to be divorced. But could I face the loneliness?"

SINGLE LIFE

Thousands opt for the single life, refusing to lose their sovereignty and freedom in a relationship they fear will absorb and strangle them with too severe a personal compromise. But they, too, know the loneliness of feeling that no one really cares whether they live or die, and the pursuit of a series of emotional and sexual contacts is often but a temporary balm, as addictive as any drug. The freedom they chose becomes another kind of prison. Many singles are still longing for the ideal relationship to save them, but gradually they grow discouraged with the reality of dating. Others believe that the search for an ideal mate is but a romantic illusion, so they finally settle for whatever friends they can find; or they simply go it alone.

ELDERLY

An increasing number of elderly citizens often feel themselves detached from the mainstream of life and cling to their pets or TVs for solace. Millions of people discover in their middle years that the skills they used for coping with life for so many decades are now ineffective and they feel powerless to start over. Unattended loneliness leads to depression and anxiety and a kind of living death. Even the traditional religions do not seem as helpful as they once were and I am increasingly conscious of the silent screams of loneliness that echo in large cities or small towns, in rural or industrial areas, in the most serene settings or in the most prosaic.

TRAPPED IN MARRIAGE

Dan, a high-school teacher, divorced his wife after three children and eleven years of marriage. Married at twenty-one and saddled with a mortgage and three infants at twenty-six, he felt that he had never "lived" at all. His wife, too, was unprepared for the sudden responsibilities, the dull routine, and never having enough money to do anything but survive. They quarreled constantly and their sex life and personal communication deteriorated. Dan started drinking and staying out and gradually got involved in a series of affairs. He lost interest in his work, home became a place of confusion and bitter quarrels, and the more he ignored his wife the more distant and distraught she became. He felt that he had never "lived" and every time he saw single people enjoying themselves, he felt a severe tension in his stomach. Every social occasion became a kind of scavenger hunt for an ideal woman. Divorce seemed to be the only answer. He moved into a small studio apartment, his wife was forced to take a job and, much to Dan's surprise, she was remarried within a year to her boss, a solid, caring man who loved her and delighted in the children.

Despite the fact that Dan had more money and endless free time after the divorce, he consistently fought bouts of depression and at one point thought of ending his own life. A year of therapy helped, but when he encountered *Search*, it was evident that his whole support system had disappeared. He had not realized that even a bad marriage gave him something to come home to. His new series of relationships seemed superficial, he had lost contact with his friends early in his marriage, and when he moved to another town four or five hours away for more excitement, the problem was only compounded. Although nice looking and in his mid-thirties, he was not prepared to cope with single life and after his initial enthusaism it became a lonely, meaningless existence. He lost the great sense of humor former friends had triggered, felt cut off from his children, was devastated by the fact that his wife could so easily find a new husband, and was sure that he had ruined any chance he had at happiness. His confidence seemed to have disappeared, he felt all women were calculating and devious, and his sense of self-worth, once strong and impermeable, was now struggling to survive. It finally became clear to him that he had lost the nourishing, supportive framework of life that gave him personal significance. He had haunted enough assorted bars and discos to realize that only increased loneliness came from seeking healing from those as wounded as he. What he was doing was looking compulsively for sexual relief from a persistent ache, rather than seeking friendship or intimacy, but even frequent sex was insignificant, confusing, and un-fulfilling.

Musings on a Napkin in a Singles Bar

Lonely eyes lining up,
  Taking what they can get,
Lonely lives signing up,
  Cling to what's left.
A hand to hold
  And silence filled with sound.
A secret told
  And a familiar smell around.
Maybe love tonight,
  An end to all the strain,
Maybe this one's right,
  And life will start again.
So many faces look the same,
  So many conversations heard before.
So many places without a name,
  So many hopes left at the door.

From *Walk Easy on the Earth*

FREEDOM FROM LOVE ADDICTION

Like thousands of others, Dan addictively thought that a

new, exciting relationship would fulfill all his needs. For a time he continued to date, took exotic vacations, drank more, played with drugs, and continued to flounder. *Search* helped him to realize that a primary relationship is often not easy to find and a personal support system has to be much broader in scope. Without a solid support system, he needed too much from his relationships and was always disappointed. He also realized that he was still in love with his wife and felt that he couldn't make it without her. On the few occasions he visited the children, he was crushed with pain in her presence. It was as if he didn't know her anymore and that she had lost all feeling for him. He hated her new husband and wanted to kill him.

Gradually his problem came into focus and he began to realize his need to build a new support system from the ground up. He needed friends, not lovers, men as well as women. He went through the painful process of deciding what he really wanted. So many decisions had been made for him early in life, so much of his life had been spent pleasing others, he didn't really understand his own wants. He later joined a church, became active in the scouts, and bought and remodeled a small house. He took an interest in his yard, went backpacking with the Sierra Club, and stopped drinking. He learned to play tennis and ski, invited friends over for dinner, and took renewed interest in his classes. He discovered that each new facet of his support system gave him more confidence and a feeling of renewed self-worth. He also spent time alone without feeling that he had to track down a woman to rescue him from it. When he last wrote to me he had met a woman he really cared about and was again enjoying his children and a warm friendship with his former wife.

AGING AND LOSS OF SUPPORT SYSTEM

The loss of a support system can be even more difficult as we age.

Martha, a fifty-four-year-old woman, finally left her husband, a dedicated alcoholic she had stopped loving ten years before.

Her social life centered around her children and grandchildren since her husband's drinking problem had severed all social contact with other couples. She had no real friends outside of her family, she had no apparent marketable skills, and she was not prepared to live alone. Even taking care of her husband as if he were a kind of naughty child had given some focus, albeit a painful one, to her life. *Search* helped her become aware of what had happened. The formation of a couple of friendships was an important beginning. Then she decided to turn her decorating skills into useful employment and to resign as the permanent babysitter for her grandchildren. An attractive woman, she gained the beginning confidence that she could build a new life.

"ONE-BASKET" SUPPORT

Many individuals have all their "supportive eggs" in one basket, not realizing that children grow up, spouses die, jobs grow dull, marriages end, and friends can grow distant or move away. Often we are not aware of how much someone means to us until it is too late.

I don't know if I love you, but without you
All my insecurities emerge like a sudden rash.
I'm not as handsome as I thought, nor as funny,
Certainly not as brilliant in my late night opinions.
No one calls the lines in my face "nature's etchings"
And I don't seem as gentle as before.
There's no one really to be angry at
And I can't seem to make anyone cry.
I didn't like my face this morning
And my shoulders weren't as broad coming from the shower.
No one smiled at my new cowboy shirt and Cheyenne boots.
I seem shorter somehow, I noticed it in the bakery window.
And there's some fear in my eyes I'm afraid everyone will see.
    Will you come back
        For a day,
        Or a weekend,

Or forever
And tell me how beautiful I am.

From *Walk Easy on the Earth*

ESSENCE OF SUPPORT SYSTEMS

Of course, the essence of a support system is to establish genuine and solid strength within oneself. All the textbooks glibly tell us this, but for the majority of us this is easier said than done. Most of us build on the love and respect we receive from others, on our work, our family, or a thousand other experiences that tell us we are worthwhile. But even love doesn't offer support if we are not able to reveal ourselves as we really are. Intimacy is based on honesty, and an intimate love can touch us at the core of our being. We do not know how to feel consistently an inner self-worth without the support of friends.

THE RAVAGING OF A SUPPORT SYSTEM

A few years ago I experienced the ravaging of my support system and the pain was the most acute I had ever experienced. I did not want to live with such intense pain. For years as a priest I had the built-in support of my Catholic parish. Later, when I was earning a doctorate in religious philosophy at Catholic University in Washington, D.C., there was tremendous camaraderie among the priest-students. It was one of the happiest periods of my life even though I had my differences with the Church. No matter where I went as a priest, every rectory across the country was like another home. When I left the priesthood, I also abandoned a powerful support network. For the most part, priests had been my only real friends, and I found it difficult to establish a similar feeling of community and caring.

Through my work as a poet and psychologist, I gradually began to sink new roots, but after a failed marriage and a growing fear of commitment, I moved frequently, looking for something I had lost in the transition from priest to layman. I continued to write successfully, but it seemed that in some way I lacked the kind of support base that had been so important and nurturing in the past. I had grown up in one house, a warm, unchanging neighborhood, a close-knit Catholic parish and school where everyone knew my first name and my athletic talents, and a beautiful Michigan city with its sloping green hills, serene lakes, and lush woods. Now, years later, my friends were scattered, my work obliged me to travel a great deal, and although I appreciated the many letters I received praising my writings, there was very little intimate and ongoing contact with these generous correspondents. But because my life was an exciting one and I received enough attention, I was able to cope successfully with the help of a few friends and an assortment of passionate hobbies and sports. Then a series of tragedies and disappointments occurred and I was emotionally devastated—I lost some seemingly unshakable inner confidence.

My older brother and closest friend, also a former priest, died of cancer within a few short months. A novel I had written about my own Irish Catholic background did not sell according to my expectations despite strong reviews. When there was interest in a mini-series developed from the novel, I spent some six months trying to write a screenplay. I moved to Los Angeles to promote the sale of the screenplay and knew the bitter frustration of thousands of writers in Hollywood. There were accolades, promises, and enthusiasm that raised my hopes, then silence and disappointment when nothing concrete ever happened. Finally, reluctantly and deeply wounded, I gave up. Another important love relationship fell apart and I began to disintegrate with it. I felt depressed and severely anxious, and I wandered in a dozen different directions. I was, in a sense, the abandoned child looking for immediate relief. As I look back, I made what appeared to be some bad decisions, but there was really nothing I could do to stem the emotional tidal wave. My support system had fallen apart. I never imagined that it could happen.

I was in good physical health and had adequate financial resources and numerous friends in different areas who were willing to help, but I didn't know how to take advantage of their assistance. I was emotionally devastated and my ego felt like a soda cracker. I did not know what to do except to work harder and ignore my feelings. A growing depression made it difficult to do anything and the attendant anxiety drained my energy. There seemed no place to go, nothing to live for. This was not a sound, logical consideration. I had a hundred places to go and a thousand reasons to live, but in the sudden explosion of my support system, I was out of balance. After several months of confusion, *Search* was born as my own way of finding relief. I began rebuilding my life's framework step by step—playing the long game. Had I anticipated all of this devastation, and I might have, I could have prepared myself for the onslaught. I could have done with relative ease what I later had to do with heroic effort.

I had to find a base, a nest, and stay in one place for a while. I had to focus all of my energies on finding the nurturing and support I needed. But it was an emergency situation, rather than a relaxed and creative effort to extend new roots. *Search* asks us to anticipate the problem, to prepare for transitions, and if we are caught unaware, as I was, it urges us to sink new roots. This can be a fearful challenge without help.

I cannot begin again
   To study the veins of granite rocks
   And explore the anxiety of clouds.
   To relearn the secrets of the trees
   And see the shadows of mountains.
There are too many forms already seen,
   Too many sounds heard too often,
   Too many dreams etched in my memory like water scarring ancient foundations.
I have already built a home in my heart
   Where sadness is only as frequent as the rain
   And joy as unpredictable as sunlight.
Come live there with me before I die of loneliness!
Beyond the curves and crest of some unwrinkled innocence,

I only want the wrinkles that I wrinkled,
I want to kiss the scars that my dagger left,
I want to see the crow's feet and to know that
    I am the crow that walked across your face.
But I cannot begin again.

From Maybe If I Loved You More

TRANSITIONS AND SUPPORT

It is almost a cliché that retirement kills more people than work and that serious depression can result from suddenly not being needed. But retirement is only one type of transition that uproots us.

Patrick, an attorney, and his wife, Jane, a marriage counselor, moved from northern to southern California to be near Patrick's parents. They had enough money to last them for several months and felt no need to start work immediately. They were excited and enthusiastic about the change, but they were not prepared for the stuffiness and seeming coldness of the community. They joined an expensive tennis club and found the members unresponsive, although the couple admitted that they themselves were not exceptionally outgoing. In their former town, they did not have to be; people came to them. Their kids found the new school undisciplined and severely cliquish and complained that they hated the town and everything about it.

Patrick discovered other changes in his life. His once passionate interest in professional sports had waned. Monday night football at his favorite bar used to keep him in enthusiastic anticipation all day, but now sports seemed insignificant. Earlier he had stopped drinking and taken up jogging, but now he had left his jogging partner behind in the move. There was no one really to laugh with like he used to. Jane missed her friends so severely that she was given to fits of crying almost every night in bed. Patrick and Jane were not set in their ways, inactive, unappealing people. They were vital and bright, capable of deep friendship and gifted in their work. Yet, they failed to realize the importance of a support system, which they had taken for granted.

In addition to friends and neighbors, they missed the house they had built with so much care, familiar landscapes, a favorite meat market, their parish church, a special trout stream, and a small lake where they went windsurfing. They were so well balanced and solid in their previous location that it never occurred to them that they were surrendering an entire way of life. Nor did they realize that it would be difficult to find the right doctor or dentist, an optometrist, a handyman, or a mechanic who could be trusted. Normal daily rudeness became a personal affront at an intersection or a movie theater or a restaurant. They talked of divorce and had reached a point of zero communication. Each blamed the other for his or her unhappiness. *Search* did not work a miracle, but it helped them to focus on their problem, which had become diffuse and confusing, and provided them with the beginning support they needed. Their marriage came back together when they realized what had happened to them. And if they ever move again, which is highly unlikely, they will know what to expect.

MOVING THROUGH LIFE'S PASSAGES

As we go through life's passages, our tastes and attitudes, our likes and dislikes can change almost imperceptibly.

George, a fabric salesman who had traveled for years and loved it, suddenly discovered that he hated to be on the road. Every motel or hotel he once delighted in seemed barren and sterile. He found it difficult to eat alone, to enjoy reading or TV in the evening. It was hard to get out of bed in the morning and his once charming personality seemed increasingly dull and lifeless. For the first time in his life he felt old and noticed the bags under his eyes. He didn't know why but he now wanted to be home every night; he did not want to leave his family and friends. At first he blamed himself for a lack of discipline and self-confidence, but through *Search* he recognized the validity of his increased need for his support system. He determined to stop traveling even if it meant working for another company.

COMPETITIVENESS

Competitiveness, which has driven so many of us through life, can be the real enemy of a support system because it reduces other people to things or obstacles. Competitiveness inhibits intimate friendship, which is the cornerstone of a support system.

Maury, a real estate broker, had made a lot of money and knew a thousand people by their first names, but when the kids grew up and his wife died of cancer, he realized that he did not have a single close friend. Maury realized that his wife had organized their social life, planned vacations, tended to his every need, and made him feel attractive, funny, and intelligent. Without her he found it impossible to take care of his laundry, knew nothing about the kitchen, and realized that he had spent his whole life acquiring and moving select rental properties. Making money was his only hobby. He was proud of his Mercedes, proud of his cabin in the mountains, and proud of his success. It had given him a kind of swagger and buoyancy, but all of this was lost in the sudden changes in his life. He felt lonely and abandoned, then depressed and hopeless in his effort to find the happiness he once knew. He made a feeble attempt on his own life. That scared him and he began the slow, often frightening prospect of rebuilding. *Search* helped him to learn something about making friends, a skill that he had ignored since he left college. After months of denial, he admitted his wife's departure had left him feeling totally abandoned and hopeless.

Since you've gone, sadness descends like thick desert air
    In an unending wave of some immobility.
There is no refreshing breeze, only the discordant screeching
    Of a blackbird in the trees.
      His throat is dry as my heart,
      His rasping as monotonous as my thoughts,
Life is an effort now, each moment of silence a scream for you.

Where did the mockingbird go?
When will the sweet water flow in spring's raging rivulets?
Please come to me early in the morning,
Come and share my bed without words or warning
Before the sun rises to announce the day
And the heat suffocates each fly and breath in its way.
A shade tree is not enough for me.
Not even cool water or a relieving breeze.
I need you moist and silent in my arms,
I need the cool sweetness of your face,
I need you before the noonday sun alarms,
Or I will die in this desert of a place.

From *Walk Easy on the Earth*

REBUILDING A SUPPORT SYSTEM

The painful reality is that we must rebuild our own support system once it has been lost. So many of us feel abandoned during the extreme crises in our lives. We were not aware of the depths of our dependency or our addictions. We want the perfect love to fill the void in our own being, or we cling to an imperfect love that is destroying us because we fear to live the life we truly want.

Susan had run from a bad relationship a dozen times, but she always came back, for financial reasons as well as emotional ones. She was not in love. She was addicted to her destructive relationship. After two or three weeks away, she felt loneliness and depression engulf her and did not have a broad enough support system to make the needed change in her life. She returned to her husband for a few days, only to feel the pressure build up to precipitate another exodus.

ADDICTIONS: ARTIFICIAL SUPPORT

Millions of people cling to their private addictions and lose themselves in the process. If they leave one relationship, they search for another to save them. *Search* asserts that only a well-rounded support system will make us free enough to have a good relationship. Many people are satisfed with fantasies and illusions about what life could be if some miracle were performed. *Searchers* take responsibility for their own lives and grow in rootedness and self-worth. A relationship that ends is not the end of our life. It is a fact that has to be faced, and it can be faced if our confidence and self-worth rest on solid ground. To find a support system within ourselves, we must become increasingly aware of what holds us together and we must develop coping skills that are not destructive. It helps to write down the elements that make up our support network and to look for weaknesses that may later cause great torment.

THE PERFECT MATE

The popular fantasy that there is an abiding romantic love relationship for everyone can be a practical dream or a destructive addiction. If we put our life on hold until we find the perfect mate, we well may be suffering from the "love addiction." Every person we meet becomes a potential mate instead of someone who has an individual identity and life independent of us. We attempt to control or manipulate them into a relationship, rather than permit love to take its rhythmic course. We go from relationship to relationship hoping that each one in turn will rescue us from an overpowering need. But if we can become reasonably whole by ourselves, with a well-balanced life of work and play, of time with friends and time apart, we well may meet another whole person who dares to do the same. In such a relationship an intimate, mutually nurturing and fulfilling love is possible.

PERSONAL COPING

I remember a glorious period in my life when I first lived in San Francisco. I scarcely dated and yet it was one of the most exciting times in my life. I bought and remodeled an old Victorian house. I went out each day to explore the city and wrote poetry in bars and parks and coffee shops. I attended political meetings, went to an assortment of growth seminars from kundalini yoga to a weird witches' coven, and engaged in conversations with everyone from longshoremen to prostitutes. When I did meet a woman I liked, I did not feel a pressing need to have her take care of me. I did my own cooking, my own laundry, worked with a carpenter to tear down walls and refurbish rooms, and walked for miles every day.

DIVORCE OR PERSONAL FULFILLMENT?

Very often individuals who feel locked in a somewhat unsatisfactory relationship can only think in terms of divorce. Yet, the economic strain, the hurt to the children, and the confusion of moving out are almost too stressful to endure.

Mary Sue, who had three young children, was married to a workaholic husband who had little or no capacity for sensitive communication. For months she struggled with the thought of divorce. After experiencing *Search*, she stopped blaming her husband for her misery and found ways to fulfill her own life rather than making a frustrating attempt to transform her mate. What he didn't provide she found in developing support seminars, in making new friendships with men and women, in becoming the person she wanted to be. Curiously, once she stopped trying to remake her husband, even their relationship improved significantly.

LAUGHTER

One of my greatest supports in life has been laughter. Modern medicine has discovered the healing power of this phenomenon, as have Norman Cousins and some creative psychologists. Life does not have to be so solemn and intense; neither does personal growth. Abundant laughter gives a new perspective to life and cleanses the spirit. I don't laugh with all of my friends, but I always need friends with whom I can laugh outrageously; these people bring out my playful side or I bring out theirs. With other friends I participate primarily in philosophical discussions or athletics; others I value because they really listen to what I am saying, or because they offer warmth and sensitivity. If we wait for the perfect relationship to save us and fulfill all of our needs, if we put all of our emotional support "in one basket," then we are likely to disintegrate when a crisis occurs that disrupts our primary relationship.

It is our own responsibility to create a substantial support system that meets our needs, no matter whom we hurt. There are thousands of people who will cling to us, drain us, agree to nurture us if we are willing to pay with our life. I am not. Neither are the countless *Searchers* I have met. If we want a rich and fulfilling life, if we want our creative energies to flow, if we want our unique genius and interior life to develop, then we have to build a support structure that frees us to be who we really are. The alternative is not to live, but to pass the time in mere existence, to join the procession of those who choose to live "lives of quiet desperation."

AXIOMS:

- Know the elements of your support system.

- Make a list of the elements of your support system and discover where it needs strengthening.

- Do not place all your support eggs in one basket.

- Addictions are not solid supports, but only temporary reliefs that imprison.

- Play the long game and build the roots that create joy and freedom and solid commitment!

A friendship like ours is without pretense or barriers,
Where no word is without consequence, no pain
    without compassion,

When time means nothing and distance is as insignificant
   as astral travel,
When a single word can sometimes say all there is to say,
And love grows organically each passing day,
Where misunderstandings are impossible
   And words have no currency,
Where a chance meeting is enough to last a lifetime,
And heart speaks to heart in a single contact.
I have known good and gentle men and women for a lifetime,
Have been bound to them by blood and debt and circumstance,
Even lashed together by work and space and passionate concern.
Yet few of these could invade the privacy of my inner being
No matter their power or brilliance, beauty or wealth.
But you were destined to reside there,
   My friend by an eternal edict,
Because even before we met,
You were already there!

From *Laughing Down Lonely Canyons*

8. Risk Taking: The Way to Personal Growth

Principle Eight: *Begin to take risks. They are the springboard to personal change and growth.*

I have always enjoyed Dear Abby's story of how she first began to write her column. Mrs. Morton Phillips, living in San Francisco as a housewife and mother with energy and ambition, read the "advice column" in the local paper and decided she could do a much better job. She contacted the editor and handed him her answers to the same questions and he agreed to read them. She left his office and hardly reached home when he called and asked for more. She took a bold risk and "Dear Abby" was born.

RISK TAKERS

Several years ago, when I lived in San Diego, a good friend of mine and his wife dropped into my beach house one Sunday morning, shared breakfast, and announced that they were going to start an apple farm in the state of Washington. It was hard to believe. Mike was a most successful advertising man who had come to southern California from Michigan, but he and his wife, Norma, were somehow dissatisfied with their lives. They were going to give up a beautiful home, a substantial income, and an ocean paradise for an unknown enterprise. Mike knew about as much about apples and farming as I did, but he and Norma had a dream. They had talked it over and planned it long enough. It was time to move and take the risk to make their dream a reality. The last I heard, their new life was more successful than they ever anticipated.

Risk taking is closely allied to building a new support system. It is often an act of courage and faith, transforming fantasy into fact. Many of us spend hours planning a move we are afraid to make. We think it out, assess the pros and cons, face the fear of possible failure, and then continue to do nothing. We can't take that "leap of faith" that can transform illusion into a whole new way of life.

Standing on the rim of the world,
Holding back, lest I fall in.
Seems like I've been here a hundred years
Telling myself
    Tomorrow I'll begin.

From *Walk Easy on the Earth*

FEAR OF LETTING GO

Risk taking is the difference between a cautious, dull, conservative life and an exciting, passionate one. We stay in a relationship that has died years ago, afraid to renew it or end it. We stick at a job we can barely tolerate, commute for hours on the freeway, fear to make new friends, deny ourselves love and adventure, because we are afraid to make that decisive move. We fear to let go and permit our own inner wisdom to guide us. I am not talking about impulsive behavior. *Searchers* evaluate taking a risk, then make a move even if all the pieces are not yet in place.

ANOTHER RISK TAKER

Frank lost an important administrative job with a wealthy foundation in the Midwest. It was anticipated that he would succeed his father, who had directed the operation for more than thirty years. He had the same kind of drive and charismatic presence, the same energy and compassion, but very little patience with the requisite politics. When he saw the handwriting on the wall, he moved to California and sold cars to support his family. He had not only never sold a car in his life, he had sold nothing since he had a paper route as a small boy. Within three months he was the leading salesman in a car dealership in southern California, where the competition was as fierce as it gets. But he did not want to be a car salesman all of his life, so he began filling the holes in his education to earn his counseling license to start a private practice.

Everyone told him it was impossible. There were already too many therapists in the area. It would be impossible to build a practice. But in his heart he believed that he had something special to offer. The car business had taught him a lot about the hurts and loneliness of people and he knew he had ability and experience from his previous work, where he arranged evening classes in an ambitious adult education system and worked with prisoners and their families in some of the most creative and intense group work ever developed within the prison system. Despite an incredible litany of personal and family problems, he eventually developed his own system of counseling, which he called the *Connective Awareness Process*, and offered a free consultation to anyone who felt they had emotional barriers to cross. He became a specialist in addictions of every variety from sex to drugs to work as a way of avoiding reality. Within two years, he had one of the most successful practices in the area.

LETTING GO OF DEPENDENCY

Frank admitted to me that for many months he hoped that someone would do all of this for him. He hoped for easy referral sources. He wondered if he should not return to the Midwest, where there was abundant psychic support and familiar territory. He had always worked for someone else, even though with his energy and creative mind he found it difficult to work under superiors and managers who lacked his own abilities. There was every reason to feel resentment and self-pity. But he took the risk and has gradually developed the kind of life that only courage could make possible.

STARTING OVER

At least a thousand people have written me or told me that a poem I wrote in *There Are Men Too Gentle to Live Among Wolves* gave them the extra burst of courage to move in a new direction. Curiously, shortly after I wrote the poem, it was included in a prominent editorial on national television that mocked the sentiments as selfish and anarchistic. But to the risk takers, the *Searchers* who found themselves in an intolerable lifestyle, even as I did, the poem became a theme song for a new life. I quote a portion of it:

It makes no sense to my friends back home
That a middle-aged man should want to roam.
But I left the money and a share of fame
And I called it quits in the business game;
I left a house and a proper wife,
    To begin to live the rest of my life . . .

It makes no sense to society
That a middle-aged man would take his leave.
The briefcase boys just shook their head,
My mother said I was better off dead.
But I packed my bag without advice
    To begin to live the rest of my life . . .

Well, I'm lonely now but my heart is free.
I enjoy a beer and watch a tree,
I can see a cloud and feel the breeze,
I can buy some bread and a bit of cheese.
And I know full well it is my right,
    To begin to live the rest of my life.

Now I have no plans for security,
No proper spouse can depend on me,
I'm not too sure of eternity,
But I know when a heart is really free.
And I walk along with a step that's light
    To begin to live the rest of my life.
                    From *There Are Men Too Gentle to Live Among Wolves*

COURAGE TO RISK

After each *Search Workshop* I have been overwhelmed at the courage individuals have demonstrated to make changes in their lives.

Marcia was abandoned by her husband and left with three children to raise. For a time she lived with her parents and licked her wounds. There seemed to be no way out of her dilemma. A series of inconsequential jobs gave her income but depressed her and made her feel worse about herself. She had married immediately after high school and had not really developed skills to do the kind of work she wanted. Somehow *Search* helped to give her the courage to earn her nursing degree, a lifelong dream, and begin life again. Now she is a nurse practitioner in northern California. She borrowed money to buy her own house and has found a man she plans to marry within the next few months.

She put her dilemma very simply. "I kept hoping that someone would rescue me, that some magic prince would pay my bills and take me and my children away from the overcrowded living conditions, the constant preoccupation with financial problems, and the drudgery of my daily life. When I decided that I had to make my own way, I began attending women's groups and taking workshops. *Search* focused in on my fear of risk taking and my childish hope that a miracle would take place. A miracle did take place but I had to make it possible.

GETTING PUBLISHED

I remember how difficult it was to sell my first book of poetry. I had moved from San Diego to Manhattan and within a few months my finances were almost depleted. Publishers were not interested in poetry. An editor at Simon and Schuster, where I had published two successful nonfiction books, reminded me that I was not Carl Sandburg or even James Dickey. He insisted that Rod McKuen was a social phenomenon and not a poet. "The American people just don't read poetry. You've got to stay in the area of writing where you have been successful." Obviously he was right, but I didn't want to write anything more about the priesthood, not at that time. I was tired of being a professional ex-priest and continued to look for cheaper housing in New York while I made every effort to sell my first book of poetry, *There Are Men Too Gentle to Live Among Wolves*.

My agents gave up. I moved to a cheap residence hotel on the West Side, where the average age was probably eighty-one. I lived in a single room with a hot-plate, ate a lot of Cheez-whiz and peanut butter, sponged meals from publishers who wanted me to write the "Son of a Modern Priest," and somehow survived. I was away from friends, from the California beaches. I was too broke to date and too proud to ask anyone for financial help, but I was determined to write what I wanted to write. My poverty and the simple life became a kind of challenge. I continued to reduce my expenses, sold my camper, and finally found a new publisher on the West Coast who was looking for authors with any kind of a reputation. He agreed to publish the book, gave me a $2500 advance, which seemed like a fortune, and *Men Too Gentle* went through six editions within twelve months. Thirty-five or forty printings later, I still remember the terror I experienced in New York. One night I had an anxiety attack that lasted for more than eight hours. I didn't know if I was going crazy or if I was dying. I could have returned to San Diego and made a decent living as a counselor, but somehow I was able to take the risk of hanging in. When I finally sold the book, I had less than $500 to my name.

FINDING THE STRENGTH

Thousands have taken similar risks. Where do we get the courage? I'm really not sure. Maybe it's stubbornness, or maybe it's some reserve strength at the core of our being. I am sure that it helps to visualize our course, to wake up each morning and forget about the past and not worry about the future, to continue to take every positive step possible toward the fulfillment of our dream. I'm not certain I could have done it if I had had a family to support, or maybe that would have made it easier. It doesn't matter since I have no way of knowing. What I do know is that a couple of friends encouraged me to hang in when all of the "practical" advice I was getting was to give it up. To attempt to be a poet in America was probably the most insane thing I ever attempted—and the most fulfilling. Years later I was able to write about the pain of rejection by dozens of publishers.

Waiting in the lobby for the big man
　To give me some time.
Waiting in the lobby for the big man
　To notice my rhyme.
He's in a meeting—very important.
　I gotta keep eating, so I wait—and wait
For the big man to give me some time.
Maybe some day I'll be a big man, and walk in—
　Hell, I'll ride in—
And the big man will leave the meeting,
　Break up the seating—
Make room for me, cuz I'm a big man
　And everybody better pay attention, please,
　And spot my creative dimension, please,
Cuz I'm a big man waiting for the big man,
　Who's probably waiting for another big man.
Which makes me realize
　I don't wanna be a big man!
From *Sunshine Days and Foggy Nights*

THE RISK OF NOT RUNNING AWAY

Risk taking does not always involve making some kind of move. At times the greatest risk is to stay where we are and not to run away.

Jess, a short, wiry gas station owner, had given up on his

marriage and felt he needed a divorce. Although he was still in love with his wife, Fran, a quiet, warm, motherly woman, he thought their marriage had grown dull and inert. Jess busied himself with the thousand and one things there are to do in the running of a gas station and auto repair facility. He often worked ten or fifteen hours a day. Even when there was nothing to do, he preferred to hang around the station rather than rush home to loneliness and boredom. Fran was as unhappy as he was, and began gaining weight. They ceased going anywhere, drifted away from their friends, and their only discussions revolved around family or financial problems. He blamed her for his unhappiness as consistently as she complained about the hours he worked. He saw himself as an elastic checkbook and she felt like a glorified maid and indentured slave.

MAKING THE FIRST MOVE

No one made the first move. Hostility, resentment, and self-pity grew proportionately. Loneliness and unexpressed anger drained their energies. Finally Jess found the strength to take the risk of communicating honestly with his spouse. He admitted his sexual estrangement and his deep unhappiness without accusing Fran. He stopped attacking her and told her how lonely and used he felt. Fortunately she was able to listen, to hear him, and to admit that she had only been feeling sorry for herself rather than getting more involved in life. She began to build a life of her own with classes, new friends, and more attention to her appearance. When she began feeling better about herself, she lost her excess weight. They took a week off by themselves and risked totally honest and direct communication since there was finally nothing more to lose. They agreed to start over, to admit what they felt, and to set aside time every day to make use of a communication technique I will explain later in this book. My last contact with them indicated that they were no longer thinking of divorce.

DIVORCE NOT ALWAYS AN ANSWER

Divorce, of course, is not the answer to every serious marital difficulty. Thousands of couples cease communicating very early in the relationship. They actually lie about their own feelings, or ignore them—which is itself a kind of lie. And if they leave a marriage, they often find that the same problem occurs in a second or a third marriage. Nothing really changes as long as they conceal their real feelings and refuse to take responsibility for their own happiness. Resentment builds, they back off from each other, and feel it is pointless to tell the truth. Soon they go their separate, lonely ways and either bury themselves in work or some other angry addiction or live in an elaborate fantasy world that promises relief without any personal effort.

FEAR OF HONEST COMMUNICATION

I often think that consistent, honest communication is the greatest risk of all, starting with an awareness of ourselves and our innermost feelings. Once we begin lying about our feelings, either actively or passively by silence, walls are built that can be torn down only with great difficulty. And curiously, we often hesitate to tell the truth because we don't want to hurt someone else. By not wanting to hurt them, we often end up causing everyone involved far more intense pain. It has become a cliché among couples that live together before marriage that the ceremony somehow changes the quality of a relationship. Others who have been married once or twice have become cynical about the possibility of any relationship surviving successfully. I don't believe the problem is with marriage. Marriage can be whatever we want it to be. We can define it for ourselves. It is honest communication that is lacking. Many of us learned early in our lives that parents and teachers did not want us to tell the truth about our feelings and subterfuge became a way of life. I have numerous friends who will tell me anything about their relationship but will not share these same confidences with their spouse. They presume that a wife or husband should be a mind reader.

CHILDREN AND RELATIONSHIPS

Don, a stocky owner of a small trucking firm, was in love with a gentle kindergarten teacher with two young girls from a previous marriage. As much as he loved her, he found it impossible to tolerate the amount of time he spent with her children. He had raised a family of four and wanted more time alone with Diane. Gradually he began to hate the weekends because it meant a picnic or a trip to Disneyland with the kids. He never really expressed his discomfort and he began subtly to back off from the relationship. He admitted that she was the most attractive person he had ever known and he was afraid to admit his deep resentment toward the girls. He enjoyed the girls for a few hours, but Diane had created a fantasy of him as superfather. She told all of her friends, usually in his presence, how great Don was with the girls. It seemed increasingly impossible for him to admit his need for time away from the children.

Search helped him to focus on his real feelings. He had been feeling guilty and selfish and was attempting to make himself more aware of the needs of the children and Diane. He forgot about himself and buried his increasing resentment. When he became sullen on a second trip to Disneyland, he admitted to Diane that the relationship wasn't working out. Her fantasy was in conflict wth his own dreams. He longed for time alone, for travel, for sensuous evenings of music and dancing and languorous love. Instead he was watching "Love Boat" and Saturday morning cartoons with the kids. Often they all had dinner or pizza together and Diane was as radiant as he was resentful. When they finally got to bed, he was no longer interested in sex and felt that he was impotent. And he was, because he had given away his power and genuine identity trying to please Diane. He admitted that it was a pattern he had followed from childhood, trying to please his parents by going to dental school. Finally he had dropped out and loved the trucking business. But the same pattern of behavior was still occurring.

He had begun to spend more time at his own home and even though he had admitted his need for time with Diane, she continually undermined his efforts with gentle requests—"You don't mind if the girls go along, do you. I just don't trust babysitters these days." Instead of telling the truth, he hedged. He discussed the babysitter issue, offered to help her find a suitable one, but usually gave in when Grandma Moses would have been suspect. Finally Don was able to admit that he had to move in a new direction. Diane had every right to be the kind of mother she wanted to be; she just had to find a man who loved spending time with her children. Don had communicated his feelings and Diane had not respected them, so he chose to respect his own needs.

PLANNING RISKS

Risk taking usually involves consideration and planning if it is to be effective. Sometimes what looks like impulsive behavior is actually the result of knowing what we want.

Nanette took a trip to Australia and married a man she had only known for three weeks. She knew exactly the kind of man she wanted and had known it for years. She was tired of the materialism that pursued her in America and dreamed of living on a ranch. After the marriage she returned home and brought her two teenaged children back with her. They were as excited as she was. Two years later she sounds as thrilled as she was when she made the decision to marry.

I want to lie with you covered with canvas in the wind,
And feel the rain beat against us.
I want to walk with you across the moor
    And feel the earth crunch under our feet,
Knowing there is no safety or security anywhere in the world
    Save in our love.

I do not want to see the sun for days,
You will be my only light, and I yours.
We will tear at each other in hunger and thirst,
Give in to our desperation, and admit finally
That we will break every law on heaven and earth
    Save the law of our love.
If you pause to think, it is too late,
If you stop to ask permission, or the least advice,
Then we must join the banality of the long line
    Walking where they are told,
Safely, securely, and sadly.

From Maybe If I Loved You More

TURNING LIFE AROUND

Changing one's whole way of life can be a powerful and liberating effort.

Gerry spent most of her life as a kind of clown, ready to laugh at anything, turning any problem into a joke. Her only mode of relating to other people was to make them laugh and she would do anything to entertain, even when it was not appropriate. She admitted that no one seemed to take her seriously, that she was really very lonely, and that her sense of humor was her way of dealing with shyness and fear of men. No one asked her out except to parties and it had been years since she had a really serious conversation with anyone. At a Stanford football game, she met a man she was attracted to and started her usual comic routine. After several minutes he said quietly, "You don't have to entertain me. I think I like you the way you are."

She couldn't handle it and felt put down. He continued to call her but she found herself afraid to go out with him. She felt like he was staring at her without her emotional clothes on. *Search* gave her enough confidence to accept his invitation and to attempt to control her wit. She began to understand that her sense of humor, when exaggerated and inappropriate, was a kind of destructive dodge of closeness. She began to take the risk of being who she really was. For weeks, her friends wondered if something was wrong and then gradually admitted that they liked the new Gerry. She still had a great sense of humor, but she did not have to be on stage on every occasion. She felt more relaxed, more herself, and the last time she wrote me she was still dating the man she met at the football game. She also admitted she had sex for the first time in several years. She had taken the risk of transforming her whole personality and given up the role of clown despite the expectations of all her friends. After a few months, no one expected her to be Joan Rivers, and her shyness became an attractive side of her new self.

LISTING RISKS

It helps to write down the risks that we would like to take and to share them with someone else. Often we have a list of things we would like to do and all we ever do is talk about them. Perhaps many of them are illusions and we can finally abandon them. Others are real and we have to take that "leap of faith" that permits us to move to a new area, to earn a degree, to change jobs, to break out of a stale relationship, to travel through Europe, to allow someone else to get close to us, to talk honestly to our parents, or, most difficult of all, to surrender to the persistent inner voice that has been telling us to change our way of life, to surrender to what is, to let go of what is destroying us.

Recently a friend of mine decided to leave her comfortable middle-class existence in the Midwest and to work in a refugee camp on the Cambodian border. She sold everything she had and just took off. The last time I talked to her she was going to return for another three months of service in Thailand. This unusual risk had given her a whole new vision of life and will probably free her to create a life far beyond her most elaborate dreams. The nice thing about taking a risk is that it leads to greater risks, to make our life the joy and wonder that it can be. A risk is an admission that life passes and can soon pass us by, that death is a boundary, and we do not have forever. It is the single most effective way to break out of a routine that is strangling us and denying us the total fulfillment that is our destiny.

AXIOMS:

- Risks are the springboard to personal growth.

- Take the ultimate risk and become who you really are.

- The risk of honest communication is perhaps the greatest source of personal growth. Stop telling lies to yourself or others.

- Take a risk and make the leap of faith that crosses the barrier of your fear.

- Play the long game and take the risks that lead to the fulfillment of dreams.

Ducks meant to fly and forage for food
Float along the lake from dock to dock,
    Barking for food and usually getting it.

Men and women meant to live and love
Sit along the lake from dock to dock,
    Sipping drinks and wondering.

From *Sunshine Days and Foggy Nights*

9. Learning to Live in the Present

Principle Nine: *Focus on the present. It's all you have.*

Hurrying through life like a child
  Forever anticipating some joy tomorrow,
  Afraid to miss something,
And missing damn near everything!
  Afraid to build a dream step by step
And to wait for all that is destined.
  Ready to take the instant pleasure lest we die
And missing all the simple beauty
  Of planting in the spring
  Harvesting in the summer
And wondering and dreaming and loving all year long.
Who will teach us to walk slowly,
    To grasp each moment,
And to understand that what now is
    Will never be again?

From *Maybe If I Loved You More*

There are periods in life when it is not difficult to live in the present. When we are passionately absorbed in our work or lost in play, when we are deeply into a relationship, communicating, making love, building a dream together, we have no difficulty remaining in the present. But as we allow our life to become more complicated, an assortment of fears and divided attention often dilutes our consciousness, depletes our strength, and diminishes our joy. We worry about financial problems, about our health or that of someone we love. We worry about children, about the economy, nuclear war, a dying friendship, or a responsibility that seems more than we can handle. Our entire focus is on the future or past failures and disappointments and we deny ourselves the beauty of the present moment.

MY PERSONAL STRUGGLE

I remember when I was a seminarian studying for the priesthood, one of my favorite spiritual writers spoke about the "sacrament of the present moment." He was attempting to make me understand that my contact with God and myself was, like any relationship, nourished and developed in the present. For me living in the present has been the most difficult of all the *Search* principles to master because I was raised in an atmosphere of anxiety wherein worry became an ingrained bad habit. Like me, many were immersed in a life structure of tension for a great part of their early life and absorbed the "worry habit" even as they did the positive things that were part of their education. Once I had been devoutly taught at home to worry about almost everything and to take responsibility for almost everyone's happiness, the process of abandoning the present was a simple one. An anxious thought would enter my mind in the midst of class or a baseball game and my mood would abruptly change from a quiet kind of peace and joy into gnawing distress. It was my inability to control the negative feelings and thoughts that destroyed my happiness.

Since I was well schooled in this process at a young age, I have struggled all my life with dozens of techniques to drag my consciousness back into the present, among them a kind of mood or thought control. When I notice a sudden mood change or energy drop, I try to be conscious of what has occurred. What was it that suddenly brought me down? Consistently, a simple thought has entered in to break my rhythm. When I am able to refocus on the present, I feel an elevation of mood and an increase of energy. It is often difficult to know whether the thought precedes the feeling or the feeling precedes the thought. I believe that it is the negative feeling that floats around looking for any thought on which to land.

HABIT OF WORRY

The habit of worry can be so all-absorbing that our whole life is lived in anxiety. We are afraid for no apparent reason because we have been taught to be afraid of life rather than to face it as it is. This habit grows massively until we are finally afflicted with anxiety when there is actually nothing real to worry about. At times it is a painful but tolerable experience. At other times, the anxiety can be so strong that it almost paralyzes us and we need temporary medical help to control our fear. But the medical help, as valuable as it is, only deals with the symptoms of our problem. The radical problem itself has to be confronted.

Several times in my life, fortunately after long intervals, I have experienced the kind of acute anxiety that almost severed me from my very consciousness and left me as an alien looking in at myself. It was as if I were finally separated from my own being through a programmed bad habit of fearing the future and ignoring the present moment. Gradually I have learned to surrender to the feeling and not merely chase away the thoughts. The feeling is energy and it will pass.

FUTURISM

One *Searcher* reported having an anxiety attack on the freeway that was so severe he was hardly able to get off. He froze at the wheel. Later he realized that he was trying to please everyone in his life but himself and had "stressed out" over future worries. Another *Searcher* admitted that she woke up in the morning with such severe anxiety that she feared a heart attack. In both cases the individuals, who knew they had no real problems that could not be faced in the present, consistently focused on future dilemmas until there was no present and seemingly no substantial hope. Such Futurizing is the focus of fear and anxiety. If we let go of the thought and surrender to the feeling, even if it takes some time, we gradually confront and conquer the fear in the present.

Increasingly, I do not think it helps to overanalyze the source, of the fear. A therapy that explains the origins of the anxiety may well be another way of continuing to focus on it without relief. After a moderate amount of understanding, I feel it is best to get on with life and learn to distract ourselves from the seemingly obsessive feeling, even as we learn to confront our fear.

Doug, a computer salesman in his early forties, admitted a similar problem at *Search*. He was able to work, to raise his family, even to pursue an active interest in sports, but the worry was always there like a black cloud that constantly took the edge off his joy.

If the anxiety is frequent and severe, some therapy can be of great help, but therapy or not, we must learn to plunge into the present moment and take action against anxiety and worry. Brooding only compounds the problem. Feeling the feeling often resolves it in time because we begin to face what we fear and know that it will pass. If it occurs when we are trying to sleep, we are as well off to get up and make a list of what we are afraid of and determine what we can do in the *present*. Brooding is destructive.

I brood too much.
You're right, it never leads anywhere.
   Nor will it.
I brood too much:
   So many hopes gone awry,
   So many reasons to cry,
   Too long alone with the sky,
      Wondering why
      Wondering why.
I brood too much.
You're right. It never leads anywhere.
Which is something else to brood about.

                   From *Walk Easy on the Earth*

BROODING VERSUS SURRENDERING

Brooding is a different experience from reflective meditation, or "processing" the feeling by permitting it to express itself and surrendering to it. When we brood, our fears parade through our consciousness like a bad movie and we fall deeper and deeper into sadness and frustration or even hopelessness and despair. Meditation or "processing" seeks gradually to cleanse our mind of negative thoughts by surrendering to our fears, or consistently ignoring them through work or diversion. Ultimately they will have to be confronted, but this does not happen all at once. Gradually we can find peace with ourselves in the present moment.

The type of meditation or method of surrender seems to depend on the individual, nor is there anything really complicated about it. We simply try whatever works for us. In the past I have experimented with "rebirthing," "touch for health," jogging, aerobics, T'ai Chi, acupuncture, hypnosis, and a variety of therapies to deal with anxiety. I am sure that each offered me some relief and insight, but for me, yoga seems to be the most effective. I relax my body on the floor by breathing deeply from the diaphragm into every crevice of my being. I experience a kind of creative visualization in which I imagine gold light entering my body through my breath and I exhale darkness and confusion. Then I do a series of recommended stretching exercises to release the various muscles in my body. In the process I seem instinctively to let go of anxiety or sadness as well.

At times, when I am relaxed, I attempt to form a picture of what my life is about or how I would like to live. I make the picture as clear and concrete as possible, and as present as possible. If I am worried about my work, I refuse to write compulsively. Instead, I picture myself at my desk writing patiently, serenely, and with abundant creativity. It is not enough to do this once. In difficult periods I may do it several times a day. If visualization is practiced regularly, the picture can be called quite rapidly into my consciousness. It is a powerful tool used effectively by thousands of people. If my work cannot be joyful and pleasurable, I do not want to do it.

If a destructive or fearful thought or feeling can lower my mood, a positive, supportive thought or feeling can elevate it. We do this almost instinctively when we anticipate some pleasure in our life. If we know that we are going to spend a weekend with good friends, play tennis, and have a barbecue, the very anticipation can elevate our mood. But ultimately, if we like our work and are reasonably happy in our relationships, it is not necessary to look forward to the weekend. We can find joy in the present moment by changing the picture that is rolling through our mind, by changing the "tape" that we are passing through our consciousness, by not dwelling on it. It works over a long period of time like magic. *Search* insists that we are in charge of our health and must find a way that works for us. But I am convinced that no matter what technique we use, it is essential to find a way to face the fear and surrender to it, or to place it in the hands of God. To be afraid of fear is to compound the problem. For years, I ran from my fears and they only grew more insistent and complex.

TAKING STOCK

At times, the problem can be more profound and we must take radical stock of our lives.

Rita spent years in a bad relationship and brooded constantly about her unhappiness and the lonely life that seemed destined to be hers. She worked part-time as a dental hygienist and had three children in their early teens. Her husband, Bob, spent most of his time fixing up old cars and testing them on weekends. There was no real life together. In her creative visualization, she saw herself surrounded by friends, enjoying plays and movies, and taking classes at the local college. She realized that she liked her work but was totally unsatisfied with her relationship. The thought of spending the rest of her life with Bob left her anxious and unhappy. Yet Rita feared to step out on her own and begin a new way of life. The loneliness and financial burden seemed overpowering and the possible effect on the children upset her terribly. For years she brooded and worried or created impossible fantasies in a kind of nonproductive daydream. When she began consistently to visualize herself as she really wanted to be and, most importantly, acted that way, she found gradual changes taking place. What she pictured in her relaxed meditation actually began to be realized, even as formerly her fears and worry usually materialized. The picture became the product, so she changed the picture.

"It was like magic," she said. In reality there was no magic or miracle about it. Through her creative visualization, Rita invaded her subconscious without probing and analyzing and began to see herself in a different light. She realized that she had been seeing herself as the pudgy, gawky child that her father had playfully criticized, hurting her very much. As long as she had that picture of herself, her only release had been empty fantasies. Some man would come along and rescue her, a diet would beautify her, or her children would grow up and she would live by herself. Through action and creative visualization Rita began to develop her own identity. She nourished her own child, loved her, praised her, recalled how loving and beautiful she was. This gave her a greater sense of self-worth and a firmer self-love. Thus she was able to make new friends; she formed a women's group to continue to elevate her own self-esteem, and she built a whole new picture of the woman she was. Most of all she lived and grew in the present. In a few months the transformation was almost unbelievable. She lost weight without trying, developed her skills as a hygienist with classes and private study, and allowed herself time away from her husband and children. She stopped focusing on and blaming her parents and her husband for their neglect and gave up the role of supermother that had caused her anger and resentment. Every day became her day and she began living in the present and creating a possible dream. She did not run from her fears but faced them and continued to nourish herself. When I last talked to Rita, she said that her relationship and sex life had improved and she and Bob were spending two weekends a month doing things together. She had stopped whining, abandoned self-pity and empty fantasies, and transformed her life by picturing creatively what she wanted it to be and actively moving toward it. Now. In the present.

ANXIETY AND WORRY

Anxiety and worry are a state of mind that reflects a basic insecurity.

Tom, a therapist and bachelor, had held his life together by work and a series of sexual partners who were willing to satisfy his bizarre tastes that included swinging and elaborate sexual fantasies. Gradually, after a *Search Workshop* and through his own form of meditation, he pictured himself as a warm, loving person who cared about the people he worked with. Clients who drove him up the wall were referred to other therapists. He stopped working on insurance disability cases that seemed to him dishonest and boring. An excellent therapist, he spent twenty minutes each morning visualizing himself working with his clients that day. He expressed his love and gratitude for their trust and truly wanted to help them. He realized that in the past he had been computing the money he would make and had lost himself in the economics of his practice. This was all part of a basic childhood fear and insecurity that he surrendered to God in his personal faith without analyzing and interpreting it. He learned at *Search* that to make money was not enough for him and that his total dissatisfaction with his work had led him into a kind of sexual addiction that compounded his unrest and did not resolve his deep, personal insecurities. His daily meditation became a kind of visual prayer and the sexual deviation took care of itself. He realized that sex was a way of avoiding closeness and diminishing his constant pain and anxiety. He was able creatively to visualize himself as the person he wanted to be and he gradually became that person in the present, not through prolonged introspection, but through living actively in the present.

When he first came to a *Search Workshop*, he admitted that he had come to find new sexual partners. When he left, he had found a few understanding friends with whom he could be honest and began the reconstruction of his own life. His work as a therapist, which he had wanted to abandon, became a loving, spiritual, intimate contact with struggling individuals who needed his support and insights. But he could not work forty hours a week to build a financial empire and allay personal fears. The change did not take place overnight, but the process of living in the present began the very day of the workshop.

AFFIRMATIONS

In addition to a morning and evening meditation, Tom also made use of affirmations or brief supportive statements. The affirmations were related to the new vision he was forming of himself: "I am a warm, loving man who cares about the people who have entrusted themselves to me"; "I am developing a loving, close relationship with a woman by actively listening and being aware of my own needs."

Affirmations tailored to our own self-image can be a most effective way of routing negative and destructive thoughts from our consciousness and bringing us back into the present. But they must be thoughts based on reality and not on wishful thinking. A therapist and *Searcher* in Texas, Jan Veltman, has written a beautiful book on affirmations for all occasions. The book is well named, *Cry Hope!*, and in it Jan reveals how her own affirmations twice brought her from despair to new wholeness—in the present. It is not merely a matter of repeating positive thoughts that challenge our negative ones. It is as important to visualize concretely what we are saying and to fashion the words that make direct contact with our fears or negative self-image, words that reflect the logical truth about ourselves. Thousands of people use affirmations every day, hundreds of times a day; the statements somehow invade their subconscious and offer them a new picture of themselves—or it at least distracts them from the negative thoughts and diminished energy and helps them get on with life.

PRAYER

Curiously, when I was a small boy saying my rosary or whispering what were called aspirations, such as "Not my will, but thine be done," these religious practices had the same effect. Sophisticates often mocked the rosary or oriental prayer beads, but in effect they are a practical way of focusing one's consciousness on the present, of controlling negative thoughts, and of surrendering one's fears and life to the God who, many believe, directs human lives. Millions still use these effective methods of keeping their relationship with God in the present. Sometimes in my morning meditation, when I am especially anxious or discouraged, I repeat over and over again, "Let go, let God!" Meanwhile I visualize myself walking serenely through the day and I sense the presence of God within me directing me in the special work that my gifts were meant to create. I don't fight my fears. I experience them and try to let go of them. At such times, I can often stop worrying about money or failure or the pain of a terminated relationship. I can accept the fact that I may never write again. My own being seems valuable and lovable whether or not I am successful and productive. Occasionally I use the rosary as I did when I was a child to involve my body in the creative transformation.

ANYTHING THAT WORKS

Actually I try anything that works because I know that ultimately I must be my own healer. As Norman Cousins put it in a lecture I attended, "Our brain is our medicine cabinet." When a practice does not work for me, no matter what it does for someone else, I abandon it. I want to remain in the present, to enjoy the work that I am doing right now, and to stop when it is time to play. Then work no longer becomes work but a kind of rhythmic self-expression. I believe our work can be play if it is a reflection of the person we really are. When I find that my writing is too slow and painful or draining and boring, I am probably not writing what I want to write. Or I am pushing too hard. I must *let go* and permit the wisdom of my own inner, spiritual being to surface. I have never been able to write someone else's book no matter how much money was involved. I can't write prose when I want to write poetry. I can't write nonfiction when my whole being demands that I write fiction. I can't write at all when I feel compelled to by some outside force or desire.

Through meditation and reflection done with creative visualization, we learn who we really are. We experience our feelings. There is no possibility of peace if our work and our loves are not an expression of our own inner being. We are living a charade of power or success or fear. Thus it is impossible to remain in the present because the present is a lie. Only the truth will set us free. "What does it profit a man if he gains the whole world and loses his own soul?"

ENMITY WITH FRIENDS

Some time ago, a dear friend stopped communicating with me. Nothing was said, but I had reason to believe that a mutual acquaintance had maligned me. The letters and phone calls stopped, my own notes were practically ignored, and even the phone call or two I initiated seemed to get a cold and perfunctory response. I felt deeply hurt and abandoned since our friendship had seemed permanent and intimate. Instead of having a confrontation, which I thought would accomplish nothing, I merely began to visualize my love for this person in the present and continued a warm contact through brief letters. I felt my pain and fear and surrendered to it. I let go of the loss. Gradually the friendship seems to be partially revitalized. Perhaps I could have brought things to a head, explained my position, and attacked the gossip monger, but for whatever reason—cowardice or wisdom—I chose not to. Even though things are not what they were, I am content to continue loving this person who is so important to me, and I believe that vindication will take place without ever having to deal with what happened. At any rate, I have brought the matter into the present, rather than denying it or raging about it, and it is no longer a source of anxiety or sadness.

REPLACING THE NEGATIVE TAPE

Learning to replace that negative tape that came from our family, our culture, our school, or perhaps our genes takes a positive effort to live as totally as we can each present moment: to observe and banish negative thoughts, or to replace them as quickly as they arise by whatever method is effective. A psychiatrist friend of mine simply yells "Stop!" when the negative tape starts to play. But this can only be a superficial palliative if we do not surrender to the feeling that is asking us to live another, more honest way. If we are working too hard or running too fast, it is likely we are avoiding a part of ourselves that we do not want to look at. Making more money or achieving more success can well be a deepening of the addiction that prevents us from enjoying the present moment, from establishing a warm and loving contact with our real, divine selves.

Dr. Ana Fleming, a psychologist friend and university lecturer in southern California, has developed an effective system of reprogramming destructive past tapes. Her method includes what she terms "objectivizing," a personal review of the events of our day in the first person. For example, "Today I got up and did my yoga stretching exercises." Then she "objectivizes" in the third person: "Ana is healthy; Ana is disciplined; Ana is healing herself; Ana is energized; Ana is alive and vital." The third-person commentary must flow logically from the autobiographical comments. The method can be practiced alone, or preferably with a friend at the same time each day.

Dr. Fleming believes that adjectives are carriers of energy

and makes liberal use of them. "It is the adjectives in our past that remain as 'receptors' in our brains and have to be replaced by constant and consistent reprogramming. If we have been called 'stupid' or 'lazy,' we continue to react to these old 'receptors' until they are replaced by new ones."

Our self-affirmations, according to Dr. Fleming, have to be based on truth and solid logic. Hence the term "objectivizing." The old receptors were the result of some significant person, usually a parent or teacher, unwittingly scarring a young brain with negative and damaging input. We must change that.

TAKING ACTION

Often I find it most helpful to take action against persistent worry or floating anxiety that focuses on undefined future fears, but I do not find it valuable to spend countless hours examining my psyche and exploring past scars with a therapist or by myself. I contact friends, walk, write, or jump into any work at hand to lose myself joyfully in what I am doing. I use meditation, the "processing" of feelings, affirmations, or creative visualization but do not prolong them endlessly. Often they give new insights, always new strength, but I do whatever it takes to turn off the negative tape. And by an all-out effort I revive the positive energy that leads to permanent wholeness. I have never been able to "think" my way out of anxiety. But if I live the way my inner being directs me to live, if I tell the truth to myself and others, no matter how difficult, the anxiety of a lifetime gradually seeps away and I feel my joy and energy rise. Frequently I ask myself, "What do I want to do at this moment?" regardless of what is expected of me.

SEARCHERS

Some people are content to live their whole lives simply by filling every moment with activity, from knitting to phone calls to TV. It is not my place to criticize them or ask them to take stock of their lives. Others like me cannot do what they do. I have been hurt enough to know that individuals survive the best way they can. *Searchers,* however, are usually more introspective, struggle with their mission in this world, and like to face life head on. They need to know that their words and work, relationships and energies are directed in a way that reflects their inner being. They realize that future fears are a smokescreen that can destroy the power of the present moment. *Searchers* do not settle easily into life and they refuse to become the victims of someone else's needs or to be satisfied with what society tells them is the good life. They examine the significance of their lives in the present moment and want their life on the outside to reflect what is taking place in the center of their souls. They have their own real values and want to live by them. Often they are at fierce odds with society's apparent values.

What of the rootless ones
   Who fail to find a place on the earth,
   Who have lost interest in Disneyland
   And don't care if the Yankees win or lose
     Or if the Jews and Arabs make peace?
Each day is a new dream too ambitious,
Each hour a new hope too capricious
    Ever to be understood.
Time is running out except for the children
   Who know life will last forever,
   Or the fearful ones who have already died.
Life has its limits too confining,
   Hope has its boundaries too defining,
    And what of the rootless ones
   Who fail to find a place on the earth?
From Walk Easy on The Earth

PAINFUL CRISIS

At times *Searchers* go through a painful crisis when a mode of living that was effective for many years no longer works.

Then they must reach down to the core of their existence and discover what has happened. At such times they can be stripped of their support system and must cling to life by a single thread. Anxiety or depression can be a daily struggle and it is essential to remain in the present moment and to build a life that is again satisfying. To lose one's self in the future or to lament the past is destructive and debilitating. The present is really all anyone has, but at times of crisis it is most difficult to remain there. Whatever it takes to live passionately in the present is ultimately a way out—even if for now the present and only passion is a game of Scrabble or a walk on the beach.

I have found in my own suffering, when nothing makes any sense and I feel that I must begin again, that the feeblest dream or desire must be developed in any way possible. We have to find some reason to go on, no matter what it takes. The healing will take place even if we begin to wonder if it ever will. No matter how many phone calls or contacts we must try, we must turn to ourselves for healing. We know more than any therapist or guru in the final analysis; we heal ourselves and determine what is or is not helpful. We will emerge as a new person from the pain that is readying us for another way of living. *Search* is no substitute for courage, but we must rediscover what we are about and take solid steps to find passion and meaning in our lives. It is not at all easy, but our hope is to find somehow a long-term, substantial way to live in the present.

Increasingly leaders in the humanistic psychological movement realize that our uncontrolled, negative thoughts destroy us and it seems almost every month that creative minds come up with new ways of living with positive energy in the present. I try everything that makes sense to me, but I know that I must remain in charge of my own health. No matter how well subscribed or widely heralded is any plan or program, it must work for me. Practical results are my criterion of truth. Many of our negative thoughts are obviously erroneous if not distorted, and sound reason can play a prominent part in our healing. The pioneering work of an Albert Ellis and a Nathaniel Branden has been most effective in this regard, helping us to see how we sabotage ourselves by letting false thinking lead us astray. The power of reason must not be ignored. There are new schools of thought that examine thought patterns and urge us to break the destructive impact of blatant criticism we have adopted as true. And the work of Alexander Lowen and bioenergetics, focusing on the body as a way to mental health, has often assisted me to remain in the present—thus the healing power of yoga or T'ai Chi or physical exercise.

Many great minds struggle with the same problem: Carl Rogers, Abraham Maslow, Rollo May, and numerous others, including the young and creative Dr. Ana Fleming. How can we replace our negative self-image with a positive one? Whatever solutions they've come up with, all seem to agree that we have to live ultimately in the present moment. It's really all we have. When we find ourselves drifting into the past to reinforce depression or looking ahead to stimulate anxiety, the present moment becomes our salvation. Maybe we can run for years, as I did, but some trauma or suffering can bring us up short and demand that we live another way. The pain, though often overwhelming, is a cleansing process that can lead us to a new and joyous self, an authentic self that will no longer tolerate charades and untruths. We wallow in the past or future and miss the creative, healing power of the present. Whatever helps, do it. No one but ourselves has the answer for us.

I forgot how beautiful it was, the spring I mean,
With daffodils strewn like careless gold nuggets
Across the ravine and purple streams of iris flowing
Suddenly overnight, a trout leaping for a May fly
At the edge of a sunlit riffle to celebrate an escape
From winter and the lonely depths of a dark reservoir
   Not unlike mine.

I forgot how beautiful it was, the spring I mean,
Amid a friend's death in December and ever new fears
Manufactured and classified jealously from everywhere
By newsmakers and baritone rumor mongers of a sad world.

Tonight when they groaned of gas shortages and suicides,
Decomposed bodies in Chicago and a dog bite in Dallas,
  I lost myself in soft rain.
I forgot how beautiful it was, the spring I mean,
And I didn't care what Texaco stole or who died in Iran,
What the dollar brought in Tokyo or land in California.
I was only grateful for green hills and a belching bullfrog,
Two deer trembling on a gravel road and a salamander
Slithering home for dinner, and wondered why I forgot
  How beautiful it was.

From Walk Easy on the Earth

My brother Dr. Philip Kavanaugh, who recently gave up a twenty-five-year psychiatric practice so that we could work more closely together on developing *Search*, maintains that therapy, like theology, can only take individuals so far in their quest for personal peace in the present moment. Like me, Dr. Phil has tried it all. He contends that when we move beyond therapy and analysis in our personal growth, therapy itself can be a deterrent and waste of time rather than a help. This from a brilliant man who has dedicated his life to therapy. According to Dr. Phil, we continue to focus on the past problem and ignore the present solution. No amount of awareness of the past is going to heal us. Many people who have had more than enough therapy will do far better through private yoga sessions, which cling to the "now," than through expensive work in therapy, which freezes the past.

As Phil and I look back over our own past, we realize that in the first period of our lives, we were permitted only theological answers. At times those answers work, but ultimately everything was God's will; our vision of life and death was as limited as that of the Catholic religion to which we gave total allegiance. In the next period of personal growth, therapy seemed the answer to everything, but in a sense, therapy was even more limited than theology. Only when we moved beyond historic theology and therapy and took responsibility for our own, present healing did we discover our personal faith and the private forms of therapy, such as yoga, meditation, and simply letting go, that free us from the prison built for us by well-meaning but short-sighted parents, priests, and teachers.

Now we are free to discover what works, and for that reason the *Search* concept will never be a static one as we move beyond traditional religion and therapy. It helps to realize that there are millions of people who have found great inner peace and fulfillment without either religion or therapy. So can we.

Many times in my life I have had a strong and powerful dream of how I wanted to live my life. Early in my adolescence the dream was as romantic and noble as were my youthful aspirations. This dream gave meaning to every day, since each hour was a step toward its fulfillment. Life and circumstances have a way of jading dreams. Ambition and pride enter in, self-righteousness and self-pity as well, and the once noble vision can become corroded with an aura of ego and self-aggrandizement. At such times the present loses its value and we can become a "house divided against itself." We rush without knowing why, accomplish without a solid awareness of our own identity, succeed when success is merely a personal sellout. Whenever I was caught in this confusion, anguish and suffering ensued, not as a punishment but as a sign that I was abusing my own being. I had lost the present in my haste to attain ambitious goals that had replaced honorable dreams. It was less my own doing than my response to what my culture and personal insecurity were constantly teaching me. Power and affluence, notoriety and recognition, images and appearance were more significant than solid integrity. The future was more important than the present. Only pain could divert me because pain was the only healer that I would finally listen to.

In later years I have been struggling to live a different way, to recapture what was lost in upward mobility. It does not matter whether one is a priest or a stockbroker, poet or contractor, obvious success or apparent failure. To lose the present moment is to lose finally a chance at joy and peace. Now I want each day to mean something, each hour to be its own reality, each step toward my dreams to be its own joy. I do not want to miss the sunsets, the laughs, the friends, the mornings, the moon. I want to be who I am at each moment of the day: joyful and sad, strong and afraid, child and man. I want to be rid of an anxiety that fears the future or a depression that laments the past. I want to see when I look, to hear when I listen, and to be grateful for each passing breath. I want to live and love in the present because it's really all I have.

AXIOMS:

- Worry is a bad habit that can be changed through re-programming.

- Replace the negative tape with a positive and logical thought.

- Live in the present. It's all you have.

- Creative visualization and personal affirmations can keep you in the present.

- Play the long game: Persist!

Well, the real estate market broke down
    And a lot of egos with it.
Paper castles came tumbling down, seaweed security
    That made us laugh at our fathers struggles
      to survive.
All blew away in some sudden wind
    from far across the globe.
Suddenly it was enough to have a house and a family,
    A tree, and a warm place by the fire.
Suddenly love meant more than all the trophies
    And accumulated equities.
So much energy spent in vacuums,
So much strength locked in file cabinets.
    So little time spent in forests
And in the quietude of our souls.

PERSONAL HAPPINESS

So much of life is spent trying to prove something. It begins in childhood and never seems to end. Trying to prove we're bigger or stronger, better or richer or smarter. Trying to prove that we deserve someone's love, but feeling secretly that we don't.

MAYBE IF I LOVED YOU MORE, I wouldn't have to prove anything.

So much of life is spent in fear. From the simple dares of childhood to the complex ones of the adult. Fear of failure, fear of losing a job or ending a relationship, fear of marriage or divorce, fear of sickness or aging, fear of love or death.

MAYBE IF I LOVED YOU MORE, I wouldn't have to be afraid.

So much of life is spent in isolation. From the lonely daydreams of a child to the unuttered secrets of an adult. Isolated in our dreams, in our thoughts, in the midst of a crowd, isolated especially in our anxieties and hurts and private rages.

MAYBE IF I LOVED YOU MORE, I wouldn't have to feel alone.

So much of life is spent in guilt. From the first sadness in a parent's eye to the tears of a lover. Guilt over working too hard or not hard enough, guilt over loving too much or not enough. Guilt over children that love us and those that don't. Guilt over money or God or our most satisfying dreams.

MAYBE IF I LOVED YOU MORE, I wouldn't have to feel guilty.

So much of life is spent in an effort to be loved. We beg for it from infancy. We struggle to please everyone, parents, teachers, neighbors, anyone who seems important. We do it all our lives. Success becomes the measure of our worth. Even the simplest failure can mean that we are not really lovable.

MAYBE IF I LOVED YOU MORE,
Finally I would be loved!

From *Maybe If I Loved You More*

10. Communication: The Art of Listening and Feeling

Principle Ten: Examine your system of communication. Do you really listen? Do you say what you are feeling?

Louise thinks
  I shouldn't take life so seriously,
  That people with fewer brains
    are a lot luckier,
  And that people who think as deeply
    as Louise thinks I sometimes do
  Create their own misery, waste a lot of time
And would be far better off having more kids,
  Or even playing cribbage.
Louise also thinks
  Her husband left her
    Because her mother and the dog
      got on his nerves,
    The kids wrecked his saw and scratched
      his Harley,
    And it snowed too much in Chicago.
Louise and I are not close.

From *Laughing Down Lonely Canyons*

"NOBODY LISTENS"

At one of my first *Search Workshops* a fiftyish woman related a story of her failed marriage in a Midwestern city. Her husband had abandoned her with three children in their teens almost ten years ago and she had not heard from him since. He had left her with a generous savings account, some income property, and had provided a trust for the children's college education.

139

He had seemingly departed without provocation or obvious preparation. He left her the late-model Pontiac he had always driven and drove off in a five-year-old Mustang with the clothes on his back, his golf clubs, and pictures of the kids. There was only a brief note that said, "Nobody listens."

Another woman in the Southwest told me the story of her father, who had divorced his wife after forty years of marriage. They were a devout Catholic family with several children and the dramatic divorce shocked the entire community. The man moved away to a neighboring town and continued to support his wife faithfully. After a couple of years he married a woman he had met at a square dance class. His only comment to his wife had been, "You always listened to the priest, but never to me."

COMMUNICATION BREAKDOWN

The demise of most substantial relationships that were destined to fall apart is the result of bad communication. Surprisingly, the communication breakdown takes place early on and as the relationship progresses, there is only perfunctory contact. When couples look back at what happened, it is difficult to know when the emotional separation occurred. It is not unusual for the change to take place on the honeymoon.

Vern felt a transition in communication at his wedding reception and by the first night of the honeymoon he knew that he could not communicate with his wife. There were signs ahead of time—he wanted a simple marriage and she talked him into her elaborate wedding fantasy, even though he was in poor health and it was a second marriage for both of them. He did not want to offend her "girlishness" and conceded. She also spent three thousand dollars more than they could afford. "I felt the marriage was over before it began," he said. "And from the day of the wedding I plotted my way out of the relationship. We just couldn't communicate."

FEAR OF COMMUNICATION

Usually one or both of the parties are afraid to say what is on their minds lest they disappoint or hurt their partner, so they retreat within themselves, feel resentment or rejection, and build protective emotional walls to survive. They talk about family problems, about new furniture or crabgrass, the kids' schoolwork, or gossip in the neighborhood, but the kind of communication that produces real intimacy is impossible. In such situations—and they are the norm rather than the exception—women usually concentrate their energies on the house or the children or spend a great deal of time on the phone and men get lost in their work or silent brooding.

Margo, an attractive brunette in her late thirties, complained of loneliness and near celibacy in her fifteen-year marriage. Rick, a box manufacturer, spent all of his time working or watching ball games; she complained that he was never home and they never did anything together. She thought she was in need of sexual counseling. She had tried new clothes, new hair styles, and new makeup, but he didn't seem to notice.

It became clear to her gradually after a workshop that they never talked to each other about anything personal. She had no idea that Rick felt isolated and rejected because all her time was spent cleaning the house and attending to three children. Nor did he realize the extent of her pain from feeling unattractive and dull. The more acute the emotional separation from each other, the harder Rick worked and the more attention Margo paid to home and children and wardrobe.

SEX AND COMMUNICATION

They did not really have a sex problem. Their sexual dilemma was only a reflection of their lack of communication, and once the chasm had been built between them, neither of them knew how to cross it. They had not only tuned each other out, but they had actually tuned out their own personal feelings. Soon they were not aware of what the problem was. Like thousands of couples, they merely lived together without the security and warmth of personal closeness. Their real lives were lived privately or with friends, because they had lied to each other during the entire marriage, lied by not saying what they were feeling. This phenomenon happens so frequently that it seems almost inevitable. After *Search* Margo took the risk of revealing herself and gave Rick the opportunity to do the same. They are discovering that their marriage is not over—it never really began.

CHILDREN AND COMMUNICATION

In a private session with them, I learned that Margo had paid so much attention to the house and children that she had no time for Rick. Soon he stopped talking about his business or his personal fears, because in the midst of every conversation, one of the kids needed a ride somewhere or Margo's girlfried called to talk endlessly about her trip to Bermuda. Margo felt used sexually because during most of her life Rick seemed to ignore her. When he made sudden overtures in bed, it seemed that she was confronted with a stranger. Rick had never really told her how much he hated the interruptions in even their most personal conversations, how deeply he felt that the kids ran their whole lives, and how angry he was that the house, girlfriends, the dog, and of course the kids took precedence over him. He had expected Margo to cross-examine his sullenness and passive withdrawal. If she did ask what was wrong, he muttered, "Nothing," and buried himself in TV or the paper.

Nor did Margo reveal her loneliness and feelings of rejection. His work seemed exciting and romantic, hers a kind of constant drudgery. She wanted him to be proud of her, to need her, to share his life with her. She had not told him this, she had merely attacked him with his absence, hoping to spend more time together. Her attack, of course, had the reverse effect, and when they did spend a weekend together, it usually proved a disappointment. Secretly they each began to fantasize a way out of the relationship. Rick wanted sexual excitement and passion again, someone who told him how wonderful he was, who listened to him and cared about what he said and did.

Margo wanted almost the same thing, and her fantasies extended to a neighbor gentleman who chatted with her over lilac trees and helped her transplant roses. She felt beautiful and feminine in his presence. Rick didn't know who Margo was and she had lost contact with him—simply because their communication had broken down.

I need to know I am loved
　Far beyond coffee in the morning and a favorite meal.
I need eyes looking at me as if there is no other left on the earth
　Words to tell me why I have been chosen from all the rest.
I need caresses, lovenotes, an arm locked in mine,
　Fingers on my face, hands brushing back my hair . . .
A love that goes all out without reservation or calculation,
　A love of total trust and total loyalty,
A love that can last until I breathe my last breath
　And gaze my last gaze—at you,
When I am finally glad that I have lived
　Because I know how much I have been loved.

From *Laughing Down Lonely Canyons*

CHILDHOOD

The inability to communicate does not usually begin with marriage; it starts somewhere in childhood and pervades our entire existence. The loving, spontaneous, excited, open child finally understands that parents and teachers do not really want to hear the truth. The manipulation and dishonesty, which are merely coping skills, begin soon after. At some point, we no longer let our parents or teachers know what we were feeling; that seemed impossible. They had an entire script according to which we were expected to live. If we ignored the script, we feared the loss of their love and respect. Parental love appeared largely conditional, so we learned to manipulate, to lie and pretend in order to be assured of some kind of acceptance. But the acceptance was not real and supportive, nor did it strengthen our self-esteem, because we were afraid to be ourselves. Some acted out their distress and became troublemakers or bad students or slid into pills and dope to cope with the pain, but most of us were docile and pleasing.

Once I smiled like a summer breeze, even in winter,
Until the seasons of my life were as monotonous
As the soft clouds and blue skies of Hawaii and the Caribbean.
I was a travel bureau, denying rain and hurricane,
Apologizing for the sudden storms that came rarely . . . .
From *Winter Has Lasted Too Long*

THE AMBIGUITY OF "I LOVE YOU"

Boys caught in the trap of pleasing exaggerated their strength and hid their sensitivity. Girls yearning to be loved and accepted learned to smile sweetly and to hide their anger or ambition. We were taught male and female roles by both our family and our culture, and even with the freedom of the sixties and seventies many of us are still caught in that relentless trap. We escape from it only when we begin to be aware of our feelings on all occasions and to express them openly.

Rick and Margo brought this entire history to their relationship. Marriage made them sure of each other as if they had purchased a piece of property. They were not really persons to each other as they had been while dating. Even then, Rick recalled, he would end up at a dull party when he wanted to walk with Margo along the beach. Any sexual experimentation ended with the wedding vows. They were man and woman, husband and wife—with all the cultural overtones contained in those words. Love itself was an ambiguous word that could mean everything from free sex to romantic dreams, from a business partnership to a substitute mother or father; nor was it ever defined. Even the words "I love you" became a source of disappointment when actions did not match Rick and Margo's separate fantasies of what love was about.

BLAMING GAME

Nor did Margo communicate openly and honestly her dissatisfaction from the very beginning of the relationship. She sought ways to manipulate Rick to get what she felt entitled to as a wife. He kept her at bay by providing the house she wanted, by giving her clothes and an occasional trip, anything to keep her from complaining, to keep her satisfied enough to let him alone and give him the space his personality required. But he never talked about his needs. He simply manipulated Margo to get them as best he could and usually felt guilty. Each of them felt justified in what they did and blamed the other for their own unhappiness. Rick was secretly hostile because he had worked hard to provide his family with all they needed and received little in return except responsibility. He privately told a friend that each sexual encounter with his wife had cost him a thousand dollars and had grown dull and perfunctory. When he introduced some erotic literature and films into their bedroom, she coldly withdrew without a word. And Margo felt that she was a slave to the house and the kids, a slavery that was not appreciated by anyone. Thus their whole life was filled with self-pity, resentment, and massive hostility. They had learned early in life not to share their real feelings lest they hurt each other or lose their partner's love. And in the process they had lost everything, because from the very beginning they had not learned to communicate honestly. Few of us do because we early on sensed that the truth was offensive to adults, who preferred to see us as an extension of themselves rather than as unique and sovereign persons.

So often I stand like a bashful child
  Speechless before those I love,
Wanting to tell them all that is in my heart,
  But frightened by some distance in their eyes.
Thus so much of life is lived all alone,
So many conversations with one's self go unanswered.
I would like to begin again, do it all right this time.
  There would be no docile, frightened adolescent,
    Smiling endlessly to hide his anger
    Trampling on his own fears
    Ignoring his private dreams

Fighting for some recognition that never came
  from within.
No one could push or prod me,
No one could intimidate or smother me . . .
Strange, even as a little boy I knew it was all wrong,
  That life was far more than docility and duty and
  self-annihilation!
All these years spent reclaiming the child who was
  Instinctively wiser than all his teachers,
All these years spent trying to recapture
  What I surrendered to frightened preachers,
Until I can only ask that the loving, prodigal child
  Who was lost will finally reappear,
So that life is the circle it was meant to be,
  That the child who flowered at life's beginning
Will once more flourish at its end.

                    From *Laughing Down Lonely Canyons*

LISTENING

Communication begins with listening, but most people do not really hear us, especially if they want something from us. They respond to the stimulus of conversation. We begin by telling about our trip to China and before we are halfway through we are sharing a friend's trip to Hawaii. Before he reaches the punchline, we reveal how much we hate cold weather. Then our friend is off on a narrative about the great ski weekend he had in Squaw Valley. We counter with a snorkeling expedition in Baja. Even when we have something on our mind, something that we really want to share with another, it is difficult to get a hearing. I remember trying to talk to a friend about my personal pain when we were sitting in a bar on Union Street in San Francisco. My words were only a backdrop to his roving eyes. It was important that he hear me, because I really needed to get some emotional relief. As often happens with some men, any attractive woman can divert their attention. Men offer each other a great insult in personal conversation when they let communication drift off in favor of a sexual appraisal of each passing waitress, or when they insist on telling success stories, as if that made them finally valuable. It is a lonely, competitive way to go, the sad residue of a masculine high-school rite of passage that can sometimes last throughout life.

Life is still
    a high school football game.
Every month
    someone new finally makes the team.
This one at fourteen,
    another at forty.

From Walk Easy on the Earth

PROFESSIONALS

Even some professionals do not necessarily listen, especially if they are seeing around thirty people a week. Or they may be listening to a therapy tape in their own head that categorizes a client according to the theories of human behavior they have adopted or inherited. We all need to be heard, especially in those relationships that are significant in our lives. There are millions of lonely people in relationships, lonely because no one really hears them or cares. And the need to be heard is strongest when we are experiencing acute pain. At such times we can be extremely draining of a friend's energy and we must be careful not to abuse a friendship, turning it into a kind of garbage disposal. Despite this caution, it is necessary to be heard by someone who really listens. We have to get it out. And to have a friend or friends who permit this is to be fortunate indeed.

LOVING SILENCE

At times it is not necessary to talk about our pain but simply to be in the presence of another person who cares. Loving silence can be a great form of communication. But there are countless human beings who have no one to talk to, let alone anyone to share a loving silence with. I will never forget a greying, thin man with the graphic marks of a long-term depression on his face who stopped by my office and asked if he could just sit near me and read. He spent the whole afternoon without asking anything but the presence of another caring person. When we finally had a chance to talk, he told a painful story of a wife who left him after he lost his job. For three years he had been surviving with part-time work, living in a shabby studio apartment without medical help or therapy and without a single friend to talk to. I told him to stop by anytime he wanted to, but I never saw him again.

EXERCISE IN LISTENING

One of the most powerful exercises we do in *Search* is to pair up and spend twenty to thirty minutes listening to another person without saying a word. I only ask that the listener give loving, compassionate, total attention. Then the roles are reversed and the listener becomes the speaker. It is essential that the listener not interrupt or even ask any questions. If the exercise becomes just another conversation it will not have the impact I want. Most of the participants have never had the experience of someone listening without interruption for thirty minutes. The rule of absolute silence prevents the listener from projecting his or her own experience on the person who is communicating. Also, most of us do not immediately talk at the level of feeling. It takes some time to reach that point and if we are interrupted, we may be diverted from ever talking about what is at the core of our being. This exercise could have great impact in helping couples to review a relationship that is deteriorating because of distance and indifference.

Often, when I am writing poetry I am filled with a strong emotion and it takes a whole page or two of writing before I reach the heart of my own experience. The first few paragraphs are filled with self-pity or confusion; then suddenly the poem begins to emerge as I finally get in touch with the truth that underlies the strong feeling. It is much the same experience in this communication exercise. Frequently people talk about something they have never really discussed with anyone before. The rule of listener silence prevents them from breaking away into superficial conversation. They may ramble for a few minutes, but usually they get in touch with something very important that they want to communicate. Frequently, two individuals who sat down as strangers rise up as beginning friends, because genuine communication is at the core of all real friendship, personal growth, and healing. A lawyer from southern California said at the end of such an exercise that he shared more with his unknown companion in a half hour than he had shared with his wife in the last five years.

COMMUNICATION AND FEELING

The ability to communicate depends on the very first *Search* principle—we have to know what we are feeling in order to reveal it. Once we are in the habit of speaking frequently at the level of feeling, a great transformation takes place in our lives. We stop lying. We realize that life is rushing by and our dreams are dissipated or dead. We have denied our fear, our disappointments, our deepest longings, or we have transformed them into nagging, bickering, or sullen silence. Meanwhile the chasm between husband and wife or friends only widens. I wrote about this at some length in *Sunshine Days and Foggy Nights*. I quote a few excerpts.

. . . Always I am afraid, afraid to lose the love I never had,
Afraid to let go of the affection I could destroy with a word.
Who has time for me as I am, rude and afraid, sullen and angry,
Listless and impetuous, silent and confused, joyful and sad?
Who has time or space unless I walk within the boundaries
   Of black or white, young or old, day or night?
. . . A million voices told me what I should want, what they wanted,
Until I didn't know what I wanted myself.
I am such futility and yet I know my futility is man,
Going where he doesn't want to go,
   Doing what he doesn't want to do,
Eating when he doesn't want to eat,
   Sexing when he doesn't want to sex.

Only afraid to be afraid, because that's what he is.
And that's who he is. And that's why it's one big lie,
Because the fear is never told and only shows in greed and fantasy,
   In emptiness and murder.
So the cosmos becomes one big bravado and frightened men
Live desperately on the earth, passing the time, denying the fear,
Till only courage and strength, success and power have currency,
And one huge lie goes from pole to pole
   While truth withers and dies, even as the men who seem to live.
For the only courage is to know I'm afraid, to begin there.
   Perhaps to end there. And never to lie again!
                    From *Sunshine Days and Foggy Nights*

AN END OF THE FAÇADE

A *Searcher* lets go of the mask, the façade, the false image
that so many people struggle to maintain at great personal cost.
To do otherwise is to battle forever vainly to establish some feeling of self-worth. If people communicate an image, they are
aware of it deep within their own consciousness, and the support or love they receive does not really touch them—only the
image. For this reason, thousands of individuals who have apparently every right to feel good about themselves, feel worthless and even suicidal. By fearing to reveal themselves and to
communicate at that level of reality, they carve a careful image
of themselves to display to the world and even to close friends.
They become the image our society thinks successful and ap-
proved. Men become what they believe women want; women
become what they think men want. Children try to please parents and parents in turn try to please children. The end result is
dishonesty and insecurity, the absence of self-love, and no one
really pleases anyone.

MOVING BEYOND THE IMAGE

Luke, a former star athlete and a handsome, outgoing man,

seemed to have abundant friends. Women pursued him because his image was that of strength and sexuality, courage and success. He revealed at *Search* that he was a lonely mannequin who feared to reveal his softness and vulnerability, his fear and sensitivity. Despite the enormous attention he received, it was only an empty fix that gave him no inner support. After a severe depression, he recognized that he had to live another way or die. Gradually he took the risk of being himself. He did not deny his strength, but he shared his sensitivity. He had become impotent trying to be superstud. When he made honest love, his body responded. He had abused himself for years with a macho image he thought others expected. In the thirty-minute communication exercise, he was able to talk about his fears and to reveal the shyness he had trampled on, to begin to present himself as he was. A massive, lifelong weight had been lifted and his sense of self-worth could finally begin to grow on a solid, honest foundation.

It is not easy to tell the truth when we have been living a lie, but it is the only way to inner peace and personal security. It could mean a change of jobs, the end or beginning of a relationship, a new set of interests and friends, but it is the start of a real life no matter what our age or experience are. It answers the profound question that most of us have been asking since childhood: "If I'm myself, will you still love me?" The truth is that only when I'm myself can I ever know love. And when I let go of my false façade, perhaps for the first time in my life I will really be able to hear someone else. I won't spend the rest of my life checking my own script or repeating my hero stories like an anxious, hungry child. I will be me. You will be you. And our honest communication will open to us a whole new world.

AXIOMS:

• Find someone who really hears you.

• Communication begins with listening.

• Release the intolerable burden of your façade.

- Communicate what you are really feeling.

- Begin now and play the long game!

How many times have I looked at you,
    And wondered where you strayed,
Wondered to what memories you wandered
    Or what secret hopes filled your heart,
Wondered in doubtful times if you wanted to leave
    To find another life where only
Gentle chimes echoed across the morning light,
    And church bells rang triumphantly at midnight.
I know I bring a fractured love,
    A heart pieced together at great cost,
Eyes scarred from too much seeing
    And ears dimmed by a plethora of sounds.
I bring you a face marked by time's relentless sculpting,
    A memory circumscribed by joy and disappointments,
A mind cluttered with unfinished plans
    And half completed hopes.
But most of all I only bring myself,
    With all the love and courage and tenderness I possess.
And I only fear when I look at you—
    withdrawn and distant—
And wonder where you strayed.

                  From *Laughing Down Lonely Canyons*

11. Freeing Ourselves From Negative People and Situations

Principle Eleven: *Free yourself from negative people and situations that sap your energy.*

I cannot look at you today.
Your eyes devour me, not with the look of freedom and friendship,
But with the stare of omnivorous eating.
Your hunger is too great, your famine too fierce.
Your lips do not taste me, you are all teeth!
Your hot breath scalds me, your tongue is savage and swordlike,
You suckle to survive. Your arms do not hold and caress,
But cling and claw, and tell me not so much that you love me,
 But that no one else should.
I feel no passion now, only gentleness.
Let me hold you, easy, like a child for a time,
And rouse in you the pride and power of your own being,
As grand and strong and beautiful as mine.
And do not hate me for what is not mine to give,
 Nor yours to take.

From *Will You Be My Friend?*

NEGATIVE POWER

I remember reading a story several years ago in San Francisco of the disturbed nun who took her mother's name in religious life and later murdered her. The details were mercifully sparse, but in my imagination I felt that the nun had entered religious life to please her mother, ignoring her own desires. Perhaps I was projecting, but sometimes the negative people in

153

our lives can be those closest to us. We succumb to their power and permit them to absorb our energy or to plan our lives. Negative forces must be resisted if we are to achieve our destiny and fulfill our private dreams. And to resist that kind of power sometimes takes all the courage we have. Millions of individuals, perhaps the majority, have lived their lives in a kind of slavery to the will of someone else. Soon this becomes a way of life and their own mission in life is destroyed by the fear of losing a love they never really had.

For years they are aware that they want another kind of life, a job that does not oppress them, a marriage or relationship that nourishes and frees them, a lifestyle that makes of each day a step toward personal fulfillment. If maturity is anything, it means to take responsibility for our own lives and to create for ourselves the kind of life that we truly want. This means that we must be in touch with our own feelings and dare to express them. When we are surrounded by negative, draining energy, we gradually lose the strength and insight to live our own lives. We lose our personal power and with it the capacity to love and grow. We are among the living dead.

THOSE CLOSE TO US

Unfortunately, negative people can be those closest to us—a parent or child, a spouse or sibling—and it often is most difficult to resist their power. It is not unusual for a parent to live out their own frustrations through their children.

Donna, a divorced woman in her mid-thirties with three children, revealed that her whole adolescence was an effort to please her mother. A once petite, attractive blonde, at her mother's insistence she entered every beauty contest that was offered in California. She practiced twirling the baton for hours and was dragged almost every weekend to some competitive event, often hours away from her home. She came in second in three beauty contests and won fourteen blue ribbons with her baton. She also grew to hate her mother and felt that her whole

adolescence was wasted trying to make her mother feel successful. Donna attributed her own divorce to a premature marriage
that seemed the only escape from her mother's power. Donna
and her mother have not spoken in nine years. And when they
had spoken before that, all they seemed to have in common
were the contests that Donna entered and almost won if the
judges hadn't been "blind as bats" and "paid off by some rich
bitch."

PARENTS

All of us would like to be close to our parents and it is worth
every effort to achieve that goal. Parents can be a great source of
support and unconditional love. They can grow in wisdom and
they can be unique confidants and best friends. Or they can be
puppeteers, narrow and cynical, guilt producers and professional complainers.

Peter, a sporting goods salesman in his late forties and a former athlete, revealed that every time he called or visited his
mother, he was forced to listen to the same complaints about
everyone in the family and how badly they treated her. At times
he wanted to scream at her: "It's no wonder! You're a bitter,
self-pitying bitch! I hate to visit you. I hate to talk to you. You
never have a kind word to say about anyone. You killed Dad
with your constant complaining, and the only reason I ever
come around is because I feel guilty if I don't."

He tried everything, even talking directly to her about her
attitude. She listened for a few moments, burst into tears, and
told him how much she had suffered to bring him into the
world. Sometimes he was able to ignore her complaints and
change the subject, but the moment there was a lull, she picked
up on her litany of woes and repeated them over and over again.
When he left her presence or got off the phone, he was totally
drained of energy and filled with a kind of helpless rage.

He finally decided to stop trying. He doesn't call anymore, or
if he does, he excuses himself as soon as she starts her bitter

complaints. He has dinner with her in a restaurant a few times a year and always makes certain that two or three other people are present so that he does not have to bear the brunt of her negative energy. At times he would like to do more for her, but he realizes that he can't. When his guilt gets the best of him, he sends her a greeting card with a hundred dollars tucked in. The real tragedy, he explained, is that she never grew wise and mellow, only old and bitter. "When I think of all the experience she has had, I regret the fact that we can't be friends. I think how wonderful it would be if I could share my problems and hopes with her. But she is totally focused on herself and will probably live forever. If she had died twenty years ago, at least I would have a few decent memories."

Looking back, Peter realized that the whole family had permitted their mother to become the whining, self-pitying monster she had evolved into. Perhaps years ago something could have been done. Now she no longer listens and any hope of a change seems impossible. Everyone loses, but Peter had to decide not to lose his own life and to be dragged down with her.

Even as I write these words I can think of numerous friends who have the same unfortunate relationship with their parents. And these are parents who have financial security, loving children, and reasonably good health, but they were never able to take responsibility for their own lives once the children left home. No amount of attention really makes anything better. So the children who are able to deal with the guilt simply move on and live their own lives. They feel the pain but they are not about to sacrifice themselves to comfort someone who cannot be comforted. The personal energy loss is too dangerous.

CHILDREN

At times it takes great courage not to be smothered by an unhappy person, even if it is our own child.

Melanie has three preteen children and the middle child, an eleven-year-old daughter, Vanessa, drove her up a wall. She had no good friends, was forever dissatisfied with school, with television, with the house they lived in, the neighborhood, their family car, her clothes, her size, and her sex, and bickered continually with her older brother and younger sister. Melanie tried everything, including compliments and every possible kindness. She tried listening to Vanessa for hours, spending more time with her than any of the other children, and taking her to professional counseling. Nothing worked. At times, she admitted, she even wished the child were dead. She worked with dieticians, holistic doctors, even astrologers and psychics. She tried to interest her in music, gymnastics, theater, sports, sewing, and horses. She sent her to a parochial school, even though the family is not Catholic, and Vanessa barely lasted three weeks. Melanie felt her energy drop to "empty" whenever she was in the presence of her daughter.

After *Search* Melanie took her daughter aside and told her point-blank that she didn't like her. She didn't want her around and she wanted to avoid her at all costs. She was tired of her complaints, of her anger and bickering, of her constant preoccupation with herself. She told her that she was going to try to make arrangements for her to live somewhere else where she might be happier. Every time the girl complained, Melanie reacted to her with her real feelings, expressing her long buried anger and disgust at the girl's behavior. When Vanessa walked into the kitchen, Melanie walked out. When the girl followed her into the living room, Melanie went for a walk. She took the other children to a movie and left Vanessa home by herself, not to punish her, she explained, but because she just couldn't stand having her around. She no longer lied about her own feelings and simply refused to put up with her. If Vanessa did not pick up her clothes, she left them on the floor. If she did not clean her room, Melanie left it the way it was. She refused to wash her clothes, to assist her in any way. And whenever possible, she stopped talking to her. She picked up a series of catalogues from boarding schools and told the daughter to choose one she wanted to go to. She kept reminding her that she didn't like her and wanted her out of the house.

It was a drastic measure that no one had suggested to

Melanie. She simply finally decided herself to get rid of the negative energy in her life even if it was caused by her own daughter. The results were unbelievable. Within three months the mother and daughter had the beginning of an entirely different relationship. Vanessa rejoined the family, began performing well in school, and became interested in cooking and dress design. In my last conversation with Melanie, she referred to the transformation as her "private miracle." The previous weekend the family had gone on a camping trip and Vanessa did all the cooking.

I would have hesitated to recommend such a means of reconciliation, but then I do not see myself as an advice guru. I never raised an eleven-year-old girl, and even if I had, I wouldn't be certain that my way was at all effective for anyone else. Melanie was weary of losing the energy and vitality that kept her life together. She had suffered enough depression and anxiety over her daughter and feared for her own mental and emotional health. Her determination to survive seems to have begun to resolve the problem.

At times the negative person can be a co-worker who drives us to distraction. As a *Searcher* we would try dialogue, understanding, or even ignoring the person, but if nothing worked, we would ultimately look for another job. To lose our energy for long periods of time is ultimately to lose our creativity and joy—if not our life. As *Searchers* we do not remain forever in a job that enervates or a relationship that tears us apart. We recognize how our love and energy can be wasted on those who only succeed in draining or even destroying us. *Searchers* do not allow guilt or manipulation to make them the victims of someone else's unhappiness, no matter how many jobs or marriages or transitions it takes.

How much love I wasted
    On those I never loved.
How much time spent in motion
    With a motionless heart,
Listening to the words

Which only echoed in the clouds.
Hoping to make amends
For what I never did.

How much love I wasted
On those I never loved,
Longing to be alone with my dreams,
Fearing to walk away
From barnacles of childhood,
Promising to return
When I had never been there at all.

A VARIETY OF ENERGY THIEVES

Often we fail to recognize an energy drain or lowered mood unless we are consistently in touch with our feelings. Not only people can drain or depress us; it can also be the house we live in, the neighborhood, our furniture, a pet who takes over the house, or an automobile we hate even though it's not yet paid for.

For years after leaving the priesthood, I found it impossible to enter a traditional church. I attended Good Friday services one afternoon in La Jolla, California, and I had to get up and leave. I left an Easter Vigil ceremony in Walnut Creek, California, when the priest joked about the symbolism of the new fire as if he were Bob Hope. One Sunday I attended church with a friend in the San Fernando Valley and the priest gave a tirade about abortion, complete with graphic details about fetuses stuffed in plastic bags. Again I had to leave. Recently, however, I attended St. Joan of Arc Church in Minneapolis, where I was asked to speak. It was an exciting experience and I felt joy and vitality in the presence of God and smiling people; my energy expanded and my happiness swelled. If I lived closer, I would love to return frequently.

For years I have found it difficult even to look at a Bible, even though I know that millions of people find great comfort there. Only gradually have I been able to read portions of the Gospels and the Old Testament Prophets without feeling anger and depression. I have had to work through the darkness of my own past and the brutal scriptural commentaries that turned love and compassion into fierce, complicated, usually meaningless dogmas. Once we become aware of our living energy, which to me is my contact with God and life, we are careful not to throw it away.

THE DRAINING TELEPHONE

If I feel consistently angry or put down around someone, I avoid them. I want to be surrounded by people who love me and whom I love. I want to feel good about myself and preserve the living energy that makes me a caring person. When energy is dissipated, creativity and joy go out the window. I recognize that I am not omnipotent, that I cannot endure all forms of pain and suffering.

This morning, for example, I felt great. Then I had a phone call from someone who had again lost a job. No matter what I suggested, it had already been tried. I kept telling myself that I was not responsible for this person's employment. I wanted to give what help I could, but this individual had innumerable resources within a rather large family; I felt used as the conversation continued. Finally I was able to say, "I'm sorry you lost your job, but I really have nothing to offer you except my sympathy and hope." A few minutes later, another person called to talk about a loneliness she was prepared to do nothing about. We spent several minutes playing what I call, "Yeah, but . . . " No matter what I suggested, she replied, "Yeah, but that didn't work." After ten minutes of "Yeah, but . . ." I was exhausted and a beautiful morning had turned into grey clouds.

Usually I know better and I don't allow my phone to become a hot line for troubled people. I know my limitations. When close friends or family members call, I accept the responsibility of my love for them and try to help in any way I can. "Come on down for a weekend! Let's see if we can't figure this thing out!" They do the same for me. But all of us can be bombarded by individuals who choose to do nothing about their empty state except drain us—if we let ourselves be drained.

CONSISTENT ANGER

When we feel consistently angry around someone, chances are the anger is coming from that person. A passive, aggressive person can beat us to death emotionally without even seeming to raise a finger. We get bombarded with a kind of subliminal hostility until we feel ourselves flattened by what is really an angry encounter. As soon as we feel our energy drop, we should ask ourselves what is taking place, then take charge of the situation and recognize that we cannot be a shoulder for the whole world to cry on.

GREAT EXPECTATIONS

Because I am a writer, I frequently receive manuscripts from individuals who want to get their work published. If it is a friend's manuscript, I either read it or admit that I don't have time. But when unsolicited manuscripts come, I have to decide whether I want to be a writer myself or a literary critic. Often the accompanying letter plucks at my guilt strings. "I know from your work and your life as a priest, that you are a very kind and considerate person and will take the time to evaluate my words." Now this is the approach of a real manipulator. I simply send the manuscript back and admit that I do not have the time. I am kind and considerate to myself as well.

INDECISION

Even friends can ask too much of us, just as we sometimes ask too much of them. But if we are really friends, we can accept a no as well as a yes. Requests to borrow money can be particularly tense. I can think of a dozen people who borrowed money from me and never paid it back. Now I make a decision: if I can afford to give the money, I do; if I can't, I tell them so or I go with them to a bank to see what kind of loan I can help them get. But in every case, I make a decision so that my energy won't be drained. Postponing painful decisions can be a brutal way of draining our energy, as in leaving letters unanswered that we don't feel ready to reply to. Now I either answer them or throw them away. I cannot tolerate the loss of power and personal peace.

John, a therapist, admitted at one of the workshops that he had fallen in love with a woman whose compulsion to be with her family drove him to distraction. When he saw her alone, their relationship was warm and nurturing. When they were involved in the family scene most weekends, he felt as tense and unhappy as she did joyous and energized. For every evening alone with Sarina, he spent time at picnics, potlucks, and Sunday brunches with the clan. Sarina honestly wanted to include him as a part of the family and was unaware of his feelings, even though he told her several times that he had no need to be a gracious stand-in at the too frequent reunions. He felt she used these gatherings as a way of avoiding closeness to him. As much as he cared for Sarina, there seemed to be no suitable way to work out the conflict and they went their separate ways. It was a painful separation, but Sarina wanted a different kind of relationship than John. Sometimes individuals who are in love hang on for years trying to resolve just such a problem that never seems to go away. John had the good sense to make up his mind in a few months that he could not emotionally afford to pay the price of Sarina's "baggage." We all bring our gathered "baggage" to any relationship and our partner has to decide, as we do, if the compromise is worth the price. John found it too great.

SEMINAR JUNKIES

At times couples remain in relationships and try everything to solve differences that simply cannot be resolved. I have acquaintances that have been going to get out of a relationship for twenty years. They seek counseling, go to seminars, try every kind of exercise, class, or sexual experiment, anything that will prevent them from recognizing that they aren't suited for each other. Years ago, in the early seventies, I wrote a popular, amusing poem that contains more than a kernel of truth.

Well, Marge girl, we've done it all!
Remember the yoga sessions—how I straightened out my spine
  Until I stretched my knee ligaments,
And then we went to the sensuality classes
And you finally had your orgasm—standing up—in line—
  Waiting to see the porno movies.
And then the two months of group sex right after
  We took the classes in learning how to fight . . .
And we confronted each other and dealt with things
  Whether we wanted to or not.
Then we went to the Jesus happening and the guitar Masses
  And I became a block captain in the twelfth precinct . . .
And I dropped out of the scouts and the rotary
  And we got our ten-speed bikes.
Then we tried massaging each other in orange flower water
  And tried 21 new positions until your back gave out . . .
Then we moved to the country, Marge, grew our own vegetables,
  Took vitamin E and learned to fly fish . . .
We brought the guru to stay with us for a month
  Until he choked while braiding his hair.
And I gave up cigarettes, girls, and then booze,
  And we both got hooked on kumquats.
Then the commune summer, the swingers' party . . .
  We sold our stocks and invested in real estate.
We stopped seeing your mother and even mine.
  Remember, Marge, remember . . .
Well now I know what it is, baby, it's you, and I'm splitting,
  Because you piss me off!

From *Faces in the City*

NEGATIVE THOUGHTS

As we have already indicated in a previous chapter, our very thoughts can be a powerful source of energy drain. As we become more perceptive of our feelings, we recognize this. We may be watching a movie, listening to the news, reading the paper, and suddenly we feel a mood change from joy to sadness or depression. Our energy has leaked out through our negative thoughts. Once we learn to control or confront these negative thoughts and feelings, we have made a great step forward. We might begin to talk not about anxiety or depression, but rather about a lack of energy. When our energy is high, so is our self-esteem. It is possible to control our negative thoughts or to replace them with positive affirmations. First, we have to become acutely aware of what takes place in our consciousness or what triggers sadness and despondency, fear and hopelessness in our subconscious. As Norman Cousins points out so well in his lectures and books, if negative thinking can upset our bodily chemistry and cause depression, hopeful, life-giving, resolute, and courageous thoughts can improve our bodily chemistry.

CONSERVING PERSONAL ENERGY

Energy is life and spirit and our most precious commodity. It can heal the illnesses of body and emotions and even our soul. We must not permit negative individuals or events to take it away, no matter the personal cost. I always enjoy watching the powerful movie *One Flew Over the Cuckoo's Nest*. In dynamic drama and symbolism, it tells us that crazy people make us crazy and healthy people make us healthy. The entire *Search* program directs us to create the healthiest kind of world in which we can live, a world where we safeguard our energy and enhance it with the right people and environment because we know that it is the source of love and personal growth. To be around loving, giving, healthy people is to become loving, giving, healthy persons ourselves.

MAKING A LIST

A helpful exercise is to make a list of the positive and negative factors in our lives, a list as long and as concrete as possible.

It should include everything from people to vacations, from the evening news and TV watching to job and recreation. We may discover surprising negative factors to eliminate, as did the couple who decided to give up watching the evening news because it depressed them and lived happier lives because of it.

Take as much time as you can with the list; it will surprise you. Then you can begin today to get rid of all the negatives, the energy-draining experiences of your life, and replace them with positive reinforcements. It may change your social life, your taste in music and art, your recreational habits, your diet, your religious affiliation, your reading habits, your neighborhood, your locale, the very climate in which you choose to live, even your marriage or your job. It well may also save your life, the only one you have.

AXIOMS:

- Recognize the loss of energy in your daily life and discover the cause.

- Energy is life and spirit, creativity and love. Energy is God.

- Create the kind of positive life you want to be most fully yourself.

- Make a careful, complete list of the positives and negatives in your life and do what you have to do to eliminate the negatives.

- Play the long game to become a vital, loving, spiritual, joyful person!

I will not be tormented by love.
There is some sickness between us
   That cannot be healed.
There are deadlines and subtle threats.
   The spontaneity is gone.
We were growing towards some union
   Beyond all words,
A commitment of our being like sea and wave,
   Growing without interference or demands.

Free to come or go, call or not call,
Nourished by some ever present thought
That found its own strength.
Now the shadow is cast for whatever reason.
Our eyes do not look like before;
You do not taste the same.
So, it's over
Because I will not be tormented by love.

From *Sunshine Days and Foggy Nights*

12. Of Personal Passion and Commitment to Our Inner Spirit

Principle Twelve: *Continue to assess feelings to know who you are and clarify goals to create genuine and passionate commitments. Be open to your inner spirit to discover your personal rhythm and mission in life.*

Of all man's gifts I admire passion most of all,
　　Passion for anything, good or evil, flesh or spirit.
I do not mean ambition and greed, commitment and creed,
　　These are man-made substitutes, passionless.
I mean a passion that forgets self and ignores time,
　　Transforming, expanding, renewing,
　　Unafraid of undoing whatever has been done.
Passion has no master or teacher, all of life is its servant,
　　It is curious about the whole world.
It lusts for sun and moon, is a friend of the stars,
　　Delights in storms and snow and the desert's heat.
No money can buy it, it is no respecter of
　　Sex or station, race or education.
Without it eyes are dim and faltering, without it
　　Death cannot come too soon.
It has already arrived, only waiting to be announced.
　　　　　　　　　　From *Walk Easy on the Earth*

WORLD OF FEELING

　　It is not unusual to meet someone, usually a man, to whom the whole world of feeling is a mystery. Don, an electrical engineer in the aerospace industry, is almost a laboratory example. As Don explained his life to me, there had never been a

167

place for feeling. Feelings had been a sign of weakness to him and even when he managed to enjoy sex, he felt nothing beyond a pleasant physical sensation. When his marriage broke up, he had such developed controls that he was able to shut out his ex-wife and children. Even when his son was involved in a serious motorcycle accident, his lifelong façade was but briefly penetrated.

In talking to him about feelings, it was like discussing color with someone blind from birth. His face was rigid, his inflection clipped and disciplined, and his body as taut as an over-inflated football. And when he began to discover that he had suppressed feelings all of his life, he was terrified to let go. He only sought help when an unexplained depression took possession of him a year after his divorce. Gradually and with effort he could express the anger and sadness that was at the core of his depression. After several months of therapy, he encountered *Search* and became one of the memorable persons that seemed totally transformed by the experience. His face looked different, his voice was softer and more resonant, but most of all, he began to express his feelings consistently for the first time in his life. He himself said that he began to see colors and hear certain sounds formerly denied him and a kind of stiffness in his hands and neck seemed to disappear. There are thousands of men and women like Don, and once they begin to feel, they enjoy almost immediately a new richness of life.

Search begins and ends with feelings. To deny or disregard them is to live a lie. It is to live with guilt and manipulation, to become someone other than who we really are. Without awareness of our feelings, we can never really know who we are and are deprived of abundant energy and joy—no matter how successful we seem to be on the surface. It is essential to recognize our feelings in every situation, especially in significant relationships. Don loved his wife and family very much, but it was as if he had never learned to speak their language. He was absolutely startled when his wife divorced him.

EXPRESSING FEELINGS

As *Searchers* we learn to express feelings, not only in family life, but in every area of our existence where it can make a positive difference. Of course, there are times when it is pointless to express our real feelings because no one wants to hear them. As is written, "Do not cast your pearls before swine."

THE ULTIMATE DENIAL

One of my closest friends denied his deepest feelings for years. He was always ready to listen to me, but he refused to share himself. In the space of a few years I watched him dissolve before my very eyes. He remained too long in an impossible relationship, he hung on to a job that never really pleased him, and a book he had worked on for many years was never published. Ultimately he died of cancer, still a relatively young man with great ability and creative genius. For whatever private reason, he refused to share his feelings with anyone and denied himself the nurturing that he desperately needed. His entire being was filled with anger and hurt, and though his wife offered him nothing, he hung onto the marriage, suffering years of pain and misunderstanding—usually with a broad, unchanging smile. Even in attempting to get his book published, he could not voice his deep disappointment but became frantic and hurried. At the end he was totally drained. During his last hours of consciousness, I asked him what really mattered in life. He looked at me sadly and said, "People!" I only wondered if he knew how much he counted and that his denial of personal feelings had cost him his life.

A NEW LIFE

For years I wondered what more I could have done. But if he chose not to open up to me, if he refused to let me share his pain and offer comfort, if he denied himself the chance to experience my love and support, there was really nothing I could do. When Carl Jung pointed out that a man in his middle years without a purpose beyond himself is destined to be neurotic, he only scratched the surface. Such a man is living death. For years, perhaps, we can pursue pleasure or power, money or attention, but there comes a time when all of that no longer matters. At such a time, we must enter the core of our being and discover a new way to live. And the new life begins with an honest awareness of our feelings.

SOMETHING TO LIVE FOR

Viktor Frankl's logotherapy, a psychological theory that seeks to explain and treat human behavior on the basis of meaning in life, originated from the author's personal observation that the Jews who survived prolonged incarceration in Hitler's death camps did so because they had something beyond themselves to live for. In the same spirit, *Search* does not end with meeting our own needs; it is but an honest beginning. As Abraham Maslow points out in his famed hierarchy of needs, when our needs are met, we have love and passion and commitment to give. We operate from a solid base of love and security and can reach out to others. In a poem I wrote, entitled "America," I stated, "Some have nothing to give. So much has been taken from them." Those who somehow survived Auschwitz had something or someone to live for, and in a sense life can be an Auschwitz for many who ignore their feelings and find nothing or no one to nourish their life. We are indeed our brother's keeper and when we are well loved and committed passionately to life, we can indeed help to save our brother in the aura of our power and love.

COMMITMENT AND THE SPIRIT OF GOD

I have always felt that there is great confusion about the word "commitment." We commit ourselves to marriage, to the priesthood, to a job, or to an endless list of responsibilities, but such commitment can be destructive if it does not reflect our growing, maturing, feeling self. I remember when I left the priesthood, many critics said quite blatantly that I had abandoned my commitment. This was never true. My commitment was to honesty and service, to joy and healing, and when I discovered that I could no longer do this work in the Church, I had to honor the more basic commitment that came from within my personal spirit. This intimate contact was my awareness of God. It is more important to me than any historic theology or legalistic ethics. When I hear the "theologians" talk about their religious theories, I am put off. It seems wordy and clumsy, an anachronistic approach to the simplicity of my own relationship with the God or spirit that lives within me and seems to guide me. In fact, as long as I was caught up in historic theology, I did not maintain satisfactory contact with the God who directed me personally. As I wrote in the Introduction to *Laughing Down Lonely Canyons*:

Gradually I have learned to believe that life is more than mere existence, that there is a subtle plan for each of us according to our individual gifts and private yearnings. There is a quiet inner rhythm guiding us once we decide to live as individuals and not remain paralyzed by the persistent threat of abandonment carried from childhood. We can cease hiding or running, face fears and persistent anxieties, and create a realistic, genuine dream no matter how long it takes. . . .

Often we abandon our dream and surrender to what seems inevitable because we have lived with childhood fantasies too grandiose ever to be realized. Ultimately we endure a marriage grown silent, work at a job we can barely tolerate, and ignore our personal feelings until we no longer really know what we want. . . . Life becomes security and survival, a painful struggle that prays for miraculous release. . . . We work harder, read more, turn to magic or illusion, sex or power or money.

This is a book for the barely brave and beginning lovers like me, who refuse to abandon their dream, now more humble and real, and struggle to meet life and even death head on. It is for those who value personal freedom as their most precious gift and want to make of life the joy it was meant to be. It is for those who refuse to give up no matter the pain, who know the worth of intimate love and friendship, and who recognize the power of God, by whatever name, that lives within us.

FALSE COMMITMENTS

To adhere to a commitment that is destroying our energy and ravaging our life force is to deny the meaning of our existence. A generation or two ago, there seemed to be no way out when divorce was a disgrace and sticking at a job for forty years was a measure of stability and courage. In the cultural upheaval of the sixties, all of our "sacred cows" were challenged. Although critics smugly classified it as the "me generation," I always took offense at their caustic and shortsighted critique. The "me generation" took personal responsibility for their own behavior. They had seen millions of Jews killed by a "we generation" who could not oppose its leaders, who sold out to authority and economic illusions. The "me generation" put an end to war and offered women and blacks a new vision of themselves. The "me generation" knew that docility and secret resentments only suffocate energy and creativity and terminate lives, and it stood up to popes and presidents, generals and slave masters of every variety. Of course, there were exaggerations. There have to be if anyone is to be heard over the din of history and the static of the status quo. But beyond the exaggerations and revolutions, there was a new personal freedom and a new respect for the individual. Millions of lives were saved from defeatism and premature death. Life did not have to be a "vale of tears."

Walk easy on the earth:
    Each life has its own fragile rhythm,
    To be aware of it is to understand,
    To ignore it is to abandon oneself to sadness.
    It is to search vainly for the wholeness
        that only comes in surrender to what is.

Walk easy on the earth:
Too much seriousness obscures beauty,

Intensity blinds and distorts one's focus,
Excessive ambition destroys true perception.
It is not hard work or suffering that debilitates,
    but a loss of contact with oneself.
Walk easy on the earth:
Anger clouds vision and rage shortens life,
Laughter is the greatest gift of the free spirit.
To laugh profoundly and often is to understand,
To laugh at oneself and all of life
    and thus to see clearly.
Walk easy on the earth:
Love is waiting to reveal itself when it is time,
Nor can one create it despite the most noble intent.
Love is the discovery of one's own rhythm in another.
Any other love regardless of time or commitment
    will only be doomed and painful.
This above all: Walk easy on the earth.

From *Walk Easy on the Earth*

BENIGN FASCISM

Commitment has been a loaded word in our culture, dipped in resentment and fear and puritanism. It has been a word to control and suppress, to inhibit freedom and to imprison spontaneity unless it was a reflection of honest growth rather than a kind of benign fascism. How could I be committed to celibacy when I had never really known a woman except my mother? How can a pregnant eighteen-year-old, embarrassed and often terrified, commit herself to a lifelong marriage when her very spouse is a mystery? Commitment does not take place at the beginning, it takes place along the way when there is a real, complete awareness of what we are committing ourselves to.

PERSONAL TRAPS

Frank, an internist, became a doctor to please his family. He wanted money and prestige and respect. He was also trapped in a superficial marriage in the expensive suburbs of Philadelphia and hung in until he felt suicidal. His marriage was not real, his profession was painful, his life seemed meaningless. He had drained so much energy from his own spirit that he had nothing to give his children. He was able to admit to me that he'd rather pump gas than prescribe another pill. He finally left the practice of medicine after twenty-one years and for the first time in his life allowed himself to be what he wanted to be, a landscape gardener, and saved his marriage as well. He is not unusual. He had never learned to assess his own needs, to listen to the spirit within himself. To remain in a marriage that is empty and meaningless is not heroism—it is the ultimate degradation. It was a denial of himself and thus a denial of the faith in God that was so much a part of his life.

Caroline raised her family by herself after her dentist husband departed early in the marriage. When the children were finally grown, she left to work in a refugee camp in Thailand, not out of guilt but out of love. She remarked that her marriage was bridge and golf, gossip and clothes—and emptiness. For some it worked, but not for Caroline. There was a deep and unyielding need to make of her life a genuine connection with God's poor. She didn't have to talk of a commitment or force herself to assist others out of guilt. She listened to her own rhythm, her own spirit, and knew that she was destined to work among the lonely and dispossessed. Her face shone when she talked about it.

THE INNER SPIRIT

There are millions of unhappy people in the world, thousands of whom have written or spoken to me, who are deaf to the spirit that speaks within them. Their road to health and contentment is not a complicated one. It begins with paying attention to their feelings and listening to their inner spirit. They listen to a thousand strident, controlling voices, or perhaps only one, who project private designs on them and make this projection a condition of loving. This process usually starts early in life when we are too fragile and needy to resist. Only the very courageous and strong can fight back. The encouraging fact is that it's really never too late. Our inner spirit and sense of rhythm does not grow finally silent unless we give up all hope. We do not have to live with regrets. We can begin listening to ourselves today and create the persistent dream that has been living with us all our lives.

DEPRESSION AND ANXIETY

Our depression and anxiety and personal pain are trying to tell us something. They were not meant to be a form of torture or discipline to make us atone for our sins. They are ultimately a benign reminder that we must move in a new direction or destroy ourselves. There is a pain that will last as long as we do until we pay attention to its eloquent message. I, like many others, have experienced it and it teases and tempts us to give up. The pain slowly begins to heal when we realize that we have refused to make decisions for our own good. The pain is able to lift us to a new level of life if we can interpret its language.

When the pain is more acute than you can bear
And you are convinced that no one in the world suffers as much,
When the morning is as opaque as night and the dawn
But a discordant alarm, announcing yet another bitter struggle
    to survive,
When a bird's song to the day or the serene murmuring of a dove
Cannot draw your mind from feeding on itself,
Clinging like some wretched scavenger to drain out joy and wonder,
. . . Know that you are not dying, but preparing to enter another level
    of life,
A level beyond avarice and fleeting fame,
Beyond servile dependence on opinions or words of praise,
Beyond power and mastery and control,
    Beyond jealousy and competition,
Beyond lust and greed and insatiable ambition,
A level where joy flows from simplicity and love,

From some rhythm shared with trees and flowers
   and circling planets.
. . . Thus pain is not an enemy but a friend who promises to take
   you where peace abides, . . .
Until you walk in the world freer and more joyful than ever before,
. . . In an harmonious accord,
   Bred of suffering and annihilation
   Bred of emptiness and frustration,
And leading directly and inexorably to a true and genuine,
   An eternal and purified self.

From Laughing Down Lonely Canyons

LISTENING TO SELF

But in order to achieve this, we have to begin listening to ourselves. At some point in my life, I stopped listening and tried to seduce my pain with whatever addiction was available and made sense: sex, power, money, work, fame, or retreat from reality. I listened to parents or teachers, persuasive and projecting friends, or the relentless brainwash of the culture. My own true values were ignored and replaced by the endless seduction of society.

. . . Life could have been easier had there been teachers
And wise men instead of drones imitating drones,
   And parrots mimicking parrots.
If I were to begin again, I would challenge authority from the crib,
Trust only smiles and laughter that echo across all darkness . . .
I woke this morning wondering what was left to do,
   Asking questions that only I can answer . . .
So for today, I will survive and for tomorrow,
Because nothing has changed from childhood,
Except I no longer permit anyone beyond myself
   To tell me what to do.

From Laughing Down Lonely Canyons

BEING IN CHARGE

I have certainly made it clear by now that *Search* is a long-range plan. The principles take time to apply consistently in our lives, but I have seen wondrous results in my own life and in the lives of many across the country. All of us are the beneficiaries and victims of our family, our education, our culture, our personal makeup, the thousands of decisions we have made in our lives, but most of us recognize only gradually that we can be in charge of our own lives. We can decide where we want to live, the kind of people we want around us, the type of work that we want to do, the kind of relationships we want to have. Failure is only a temporary setback. Pain does pass even though it seems that it never will. *Search* encourages us to take no more self-destructive steps.

SELF-AWARENESS

Each of the principles increases our self-awareness. Life no longer becomes an accident. We stop complaining about the past or fretting about the future. Each period of our life has its own understanding. Each crisis can be a determination to grow, but we have to create the circumstances that make growth possible. We have to learn the coping skills that enable us to become the person we are capable of being. I can look back on my life and remember how I permitted myself to be controlled by whatever addiction that seemed a shortcut to my own happiness. *Search* asks that we move beyond shortcuts, that each principle become a measure of the continuing process of growth. We will simplify our lives, rid ourselves of the negative and destructive forces that have made us unhappy, learn to make decisions in our own favor, determine to meet our own needs so that we will have the energy to create a full and loving and committed life.

THE MIRACLE OF LIFE

I doubt that ever before in human history have so many individuals been ready to realize their full potential, to ask of life "everything good and beautiful that it can provide." Fewer of us stumble through life anymore, and if we are confused and troubled, there is a place to go to get the kind of help that we need. If we do not give up, if we are not afraid to respect our feelings and tell the truth, if we are not overwhelmed by pain or stress, fatigue or failure, if we are not afraid to reach out to others and find the nurturing, the love, the intimacy that makes of life the miracle that it can be.

THE GOD WITHIN

I have made a lot of mistakes in my life, bad decisions, faulty judgments, disappointing pursuits. I have let others decide what is best for me. I have sacrificed my own happiness and dreams to fulfill the dreams of others. I did it because I was hungry for love and did not really believe that if I were my true and honest self, love would be my birthright. In the complications of religious dogma and rigid ethics, historical accretions and stringent superstitions, I lost contact with the God who lives within me. Now in my private prayer and meditation, in my frequent affirmations and reflections, I ask for guidance and direction. I ask that my life may become what my God, my inner spirit wants it to be. I gradually recognize my special gifts and want to use them for my own joy and the good of others. I try to understand pain as a process of purification and personal insecurity as a lack of abiding faith. My relationship with God is direct and simple, even when I find it hard to remain in contact. I appreciate the experience that has taught me the futility of empty and vain pursuits, and I truly believe that I was destined to be a loving, giving, joyful, child of God.

SEARCH

Search is a positive, practical way to ensure that we emerge as individuals, committed to the goals that express our own beauty, our special creativity, our divine uniqueness. It is not a master plan or some inspired program from on high. It is a simple, clear, evolving, and direct way to release a man or woman from the negative and destructive forces that keep us locked in a prison of someone else's making. *Search* encourages and teaches us to become a part of life's plan, flowing with its rhythm, continually discovering ourselves, ever more aware of the beauty that is within us and everywhere around us. If we do not belong to ourselves, we belong to no one. We must realize that we are finally in charge. *Search*, like any other help along the often confusing way, can only be a guide "for those who dare to ask of life everything good and beautiful."

As I try to live by its principles, I have a vision of growing older, not to see life and joy slip away, but to build a world around me that is a reflection of everything I want from life: a world of love and joy, compassion and wonder, fulfillment and peace.

When I grey, I want the young to laugh and ask questions.
I want the deer to nibble grass by the lake at twilight,
And mallards to circle my pond cautiously at sunrise.
I want to gaze at mountains I have climbed
And dream of all the cities I have seen at midnight.
I want to remember every love like a familiar landscape,
And write the stories I had forgotten in life's haste.
I want to sit with you in silence, share a thousand dreams
    without a word,
I want to be friends with the whole world and a gentle guest
    of all the universe.

Most of all, when I grey, I want to be grateful for every breath,
    forgiving of every least injury,
Mindful of everyone I've hurt and thankful for everyone
    who ever loved me.

When I grey, I want the days to blend softly into night,
The darkness to surrender patiently to dawn.
I want to shout the history of my joys from hilltops,
And sing a new and passionate and never-ending song.
I want to laugh with lifelong friends at table,
To exaggerate our triumphs drinking wine,

I want to write as long as I am able,
And thank the household gods that you are mine.

When I grey.

From *Laughing Down Lonely Canyons*

ON COURSE

An unrealistic and artificial commitment does not reflect who we are and is destructive of our potential and integrity as a person. It is a most uncreative and unspiritual act no matter how noble or self-sacrificing it may appear on the surface. True passion, honest commitment, and abundant energy are the organic result of the application of the *Search* principles in our lives. Our very being tells us when we are on course if we listen. And our inner spirit, the God within, is the ultimate guide "for those who dare to ask of life everything good and beautiful."

I will never forget a cab ride I took one night after delicious gumbo in a New Orleans hideaway. A laughing black grandmother took me slowly back to my hotel. She told me about the two grandchildren that were living with her since her daughter's marriage broke up. She told me of the wonder of meeting new people every day, of comforting the sad ones and sharing joy with the happy ones. She told me how grateful she was for enough to eat, a job she loved, a city that delighted her, and a world that offered her an endless parade of beauty. Her two marriages hadn't worked out and there was a time when blacks hadn't fared so well, but none of this had made her bitter or depressed. Life was very much today. She drove long hours and felt the pinch of difficult economic times, but she radiated a joy that filled the cab and my being as well. I doubt she'll ever encounter *Search*, but I often think of her and the wondrous time we shared whenever I am confused about my personal search. She is a kind of symbol to me that we create our own lives, our own fulfillment, our own joy. I hope that this book can in some way contribute to your own positive search, so that you, like her, may "dare to ask of life everything good and beautiful."

AXIOMS:

- Continue to assess feelings to know who you are.

- Continue to clarify goals to create the life you want.

- The goal of *Search* is to create passionate commitments that truly reflect who you are.

- When your own needs are met, find a reason to live that extends beyond yourself.

- Communicating with your inner spirit (the God within) is the source of strength and insight into your special mission in life.

- Play the long game to realize your unique beauty and creativity!

Epilogue

Once, at a difficult period of my life, when my marriage had ended and the priesthood was far behind me, I spent several months alone in a house that overlooked the ocean. I knew it was a time to grow, to get reacquainted with myself, and to discover the shadows of my own soul. Perhaps it was the first time in my life that I realized at any genuine level that I had to create my own world. Perhaps *Search* was born at that moment in my life.

I knew that the support system that had sustained me in the past was no longer available, and leaving the priesthood meant leaving lifelong friends as well. I felt sad that my marriage had not worked out, and I looked forward to the day when my life would come together. I began to realize that ten years in the seminary and as many years in the priesthood had not really prepared me for the world. I was still a beginner at life.

Poetry was a kind companion when there was no one else to talk to and I started my second book at that time. One morning, from my own longing for closeness, I wrote a poem that became the title poem of that book, *Will You Be My Friend?* It is now the poem with which I end every *Search Workshop* because I recognize that the search really begins and ends with love. And friendship is the very core of love. It is strange how the poem was produced. It wrote itself as poems sometimes do, so I always felt that it was more than mine, that in some curious way it belonged to some universal consciousness. It flowed easily without thought or editing. It is a gift that someone gave to me, and I would like to share it with you.

Will you be my friend?
There are so many reasons why you never should:
I'm sometimes sullen, often shy, acutely sensitive,

182

My fear erupts as anger, I find it hard to give,
I talk about myself when I'm afraid,
And often spend a day without anything to say.
   But I will make you laugh and love you quite a bit,
   And hold you when you're sad.
I cry a little almost every day
Because I'm more caring than strangers ever know,
And if at times I show my tender side,
(The soft and warmer part I hide)
I wonder
   Will you be my friend?
A friend
   Who far beyond the feebleness of any vow or tie
   Will touch the secret place where I am really I,
   To know the pain of lips that plead and eyes that weep,
   Who will not run away when you find me in the street
   Alone—and lying mangled by my quota of defeats
   But will stop and stay and tell me of another day
   When I was beautiful.

Will you be my friend?
There are so many reasons why you never should:
Often I'm too serious, seldom predictably the same,
Sometimes cold and distant, probably I'll always change.
I bluster and brag, seek attention like a child,
I brood and pout, my anger can be wild,
   But I will make you laugh and love you quite a bit
   And be near when you're afraid.
I shake a little almost every day
Because I'm more frightened than strangers ever know
And if at times I show my trembling side
(The anxious, fearful part I hide)
I wonder
   Will you be my friend?

A friend
   Who when I fear your closeness feels me push away
   And stubbornly will stay to share what's left on such a day,
   Who when no one knows my name or calls me on the phone,
   When there's no concern for me—what I have or haven't done—

And those I've helped and counted on have, oh so deftly, run,
Who when there's nothing left but me, stripped of charm and
subtlety,
Will nonetheless remain.

Will you be my friend?
For no reason that I know
Except I want you so.

From *Will You Be My Friend?*

Appendix: The Search Workshop

With the help of the *Search* book and someone qualified to act as leader, it is my hope that *Search* can be offered throughout the country so that thousands will have the opportunity to experience the impact of the workshop. It could be held at someone's home on a weekend or for four weekly meetings each of which would cover three of the twelve principles. Thereafter monthly meetings would reinforce the principles and deepen the support and friendship.

The ideal number of participants is from twelve to twenty in a private setting, although we now prefer a somewhat larger group at the Institute. Each participant should have a copy of this book. The task of the leader is to keep people on track, to make certain that there is a positive attitude maintained throughout, and that the group does not get involved in "personal problem solving" or "therapy." This does not mean that the input of individuals is not welcome. It is actually essential, but the primary goal is the personal understanding and application of the principles. The leader is not expected to be a professional counselor, although that could be helpful if the workshop does not end up as a group therapy session. The leader is not a guru, but a director, a facilitator, a fellow participant— assuredly not a dictator.

The Institute will be happy to provide a workbook and cassettes, even a videocassette of James Kavanaugh talking about *Search* if the group finds that helpful. The cost of the materials can be paid by the participants. It would undoubtedly be helpful but certainly not essential for the leader to have taken a workshop at the Institute, since we are not trying to keep a solid, helpful idea to ourselves, franchise a business, or create a massive money-making program. We want *Search* available to as many people as possible, and even though reading the book can be a profound growth experience in itself, the presence of other individuals in a group setting will lend strength and breadth to the program. It will also be the beginning of establishing a growing support system of special people in an area.

Group leaders can contact us and we will let them know of other *Search* groups and Institute members in a locale; gradually a solid network of *Searchers* can be formed. There are so many lonely, sensitive, searching individuals throughout the country that *Search* can be a real source of personal contact, mutual support, and the formation of lasting friendships. We have made it clear that *Search* is not therapy, that it is for healthy people looking for a life plan. We have discovered that there are thousands of men and women who want to move through a painful transition into a fuller, more complete life. They want life to mean much more than it does. They may have experienced grief or sadness, depression or anxiety, or simply a kind of personal emptiness and loneliness. They need the direction and encouragement that *Search* provides. They need to know that there are other people like themselves who have much love and nourishment to offer. It is not necessary to go it alone.

We need each other often desperately. When marriages end or families grow up and leave, we need to replace this root support with something new and substantial. We were not destined to struggle all by ourselves, even if at the core of our being we have to find our own way and learn to nurture and support ourselves. At times we do not have the intimate love relationship that gives meaning to our lives. We do not have the courage to seek a new job or new way of life all by ourselves. Our neighborhood, our church, our local community is often not enough. We need a greater degree of reflection, learning, and intimacy. We need to create a solid plan to continue to grow, a way to live our lives fully and passionately. The changes that I have witnessed in individuals who have attended *Search Workshops* have been often remarkable. I want as many as possible to share in that experience. And through the *Search* book and the Institute, through the workbook and cassettes, we are trying to make this program as available to as many individuals as possible.

Poetry can be a great help in assisting the participants to get in touch with their own feelings and to relieve the intensity of the workshop. We recommend frequent breaks so that individuals have time to communicate privately. We also recommend breaking the group up in twos or threes for several of the exercises. This helps to create a feeling of comfort and to dissipate anxiety. It is also most helpful at the beginning of the group to permit members to talk a bit about themselves and what they are looking for. This is explained in more detail in the workbook and cassettes. It is not essential to use the poetry that has been provided in the *Search* book, although this material has proven helpful; other favorite poems may be selected—whatever works.

For additional information on *Search Workshops*, address The Kavanaugh Institute, P.O. Drawer 1719, Laguna Beach, CA 92652.

I look forward to the day when I can visit large *Search* organizations in my travels, read a little poetry, and share the joys and pain of my own personal struggles to become a loving, caring, creative, joyful human being. After all, what else is there? For whatever reason, my own life has been a strange kind of odyssey that somehow is reflected in thousands of other lives. There are so many of us trying to live profoundly in touch with our own spirit, the spirit of God by whatever name that dwells within us. It is my profound hope that this book will reach the individuals it is supposed to reach, that all of us may find the peace and joy we deserve, and that our world, the world that we have created, will offer us a loving, nurturing, gentle home in which we can live.

Let go of it all and see where it takes you!
Let the money slide away and the tense entrepreneurs

Who talk of conquests and security.
Let the cars whiz by with their square jaws and unseeing eyes.
Let go of it all and lie on the ground to taste the sweetness
　Of dirt and make best friends with the protective fog.
Toss your plans aboard the first breeze heading far north
　And your ambitions on a breeze heading deep south.
Let life descend upon you like lava and sunshine
　And let the clouds guide you as they will.
There's no mountain high enough to climb with final satisfaction,
　No ocean vast enough to cross with ultimate joy.
There is only laughter and peace, your own breath singing
　In unison with the throbbing melody of the earth,
Your own flight as aimless and transient as the birds.
　Let it all go and wash you like the rain!
　Let it all go and buffet you like the wind.
　Let it all go, and see where it takes you
Until you are one with the earth and all its inhabitants,
　And finally one with yourself!